Presented
to

_____

by

_____

_____
Date

_____
Occasion

Table Of Contents

The Salvation Experience — 7

Your Business Decisions

1. When You Are Asked To Participate In Unscrupulous Business Activities — 11
2. When You Face Unfair Complaints Or Criticism — 15
3. When Your Business Is Failing — 19
4. When You Face A Hostile Board — 23
5. When A Business Deal Falls Through — 27
6. When Your Partnership Is Threatened — 31
7. When You Want To Change Your Profession — 35
8. When You Start A New Business — 39
9. When Your Competitor Has An Advantage Over You — 42

Your Customers

10. When A Customer Is Dissatisfied — 46
11. When A Customer Offends You — 49
12. When A Customer Refuses To Pay You — 52
13. When A Customer Deceives You — 55
14. When A Customer Becomes A Nuisance — 58
15. When A Customer Is Dishonest — 61
16. When A Customer Embarrasses You — 64
17. When A Customer Takes You To Court — 68

Your Daily Schedule

18	When You Feel Disorganized	72
19	When Your Day Falls Apart	76
20	When Your Schedule Is Overbooked	80
21	When You Face Constant Interruptions	83
22	When You Need A Break	86

Your Employees

23	When Your Employee Disappoints You	89
24	When Your Employee Cheats You	92
25	When Your Employee Makes A Costly Error	95
26	When Your Employee Slanders You	98
27	When Your Employee Is Hurting	101
28	When Your Employee Has A Personal Crisis	105
29	When Your Employees Lack Your Passion	108
30	When You Want To Motivate Your Staff	111
31	When Your Employee Faces Termination	114
32	When You Lose A Key Employee	118
33	When A Colleague Needs Your Support	121
34	When Your Instructions Are Ignored	124

Your Employer

35	When Your Employer Seems Uncompassionate	126
36	When Your Employer Creates Your Stress	130

4 ▪ Table Of Contents

37	When Your Employer Disappoints You	133
38	When You Have Made A Costly Mistake	137
39	When You Feel Unqualified	141

Your Family

40	When You Face Marital Problems	145
41	When Your Spouse Is Unsupportive	149
42	When A Family Member Faces Sickness	153
43	When Your Family Time Is Inadequate	156
44	When Your Work Schedule Interferes With Your Spiritual Life	159

Your Finances

45	When It Seems Impossible To Pay Your Bills	163
46	When You Need A Financial Plan	167
47	When You Face A Volatile Economy	171
48	When You Are Tempted Toward Dishonesty	175
49	When Tithing Seems Too Difficult	180
50	When You Want To Generate Venture Capital	185
51	When You Want To Retire	188

Your Stress

52	When You Have Been Deceived	192
53	When You Feel Betrayed	196
54	When You Experience Jealousy Towards The Success Of Others	200

55	When You Feel Used	203
56	When You Face Litigation	206
57	When Tragedy Strikes	210
58	When You Feel Overworked	214
59	When You Experience Burnout And Loss Of Interest	218
60	When You Feel Threatened	220
61	When You Feel Like Giving Up	224
62	When You Do Not Feel God's Presence	227
63	When You Have Bad Memories Of The Past	231
64	When Slanderous Remarks Circulate Your Office	235

Your Wisdom

65	Achievement	238
66	Ambition	240
67	Anger	243
68	Comfort	246
69	Commitment	250
70	Compromising	253
71	Counsel	257
72	Decisiveness	260
73	Depression	262
74	Diligence	265
75	Encouragement	268
76	Faith	272
77	Favor	277
78	Forgiveness	280
79	Goal-Setting	283

Table Of Contents

80	Healing	286
81	Honesty	291
82	Ideas	295
83	Integrity	298
84	Leadership	301
85	Loneliness	304
86	Love	308
87	Loyalty	314
88	Motivation	317
89	Negotiation	321
90	Obedience	325
91	Patience	330
92	Peace	333
93	Praise	336
94	Prayer	341
95	Protection	345
96	Respect	349
97	Self-Control	351
98	Servant's Heart	354
99	Strength	358
100	Wisdom	362
101	Word Of God	366

101 Wisdom Keys — 371
31 Facts About Wisdom — 378

The Businessman's Topical Bible · ISBN 1-56394-167-8/B-33
Copyright © 2002 by **MIKE MURDOCK**
All publishing rights belong exclusively to Wisdom International
Published by The Wisdom Center · P. O. Box 99 · Denton, TX 76202
1-888-WISDOM-1 (1-888-947-3661) · Website: www.thewisdomcenter.tv
Unless otherwise indicated, all Scripture quotations are taken from the King James Version of the Bible. Printed in the United States of America. All rights reserved under International Copyright Law. Contents and/or cover may not be reproduced in whole or in part in any form without the express written consent of the Publisher.   0703010k

The Salvation Experience

There Are 3 Basic Reasons To Believe The Bible Is The Infallible And Pure Word Of God

1. *No Human Would Have Written A Standard This High.* Think of the best person you know. You must admit, he would have left certain scriptures out had he written the Bible. So the Bible projects a super human standard and way of life. It has to be God. No man you know would have ever written a standard this high.

2. *There Is An Aura, A Presence The Bible Generates Which No Other Book In The World Creates.* Lay an encyclopedia on your table at the restaurant. Nobody will look at you twice. But when you lay the Bible on the table, they will stare at you, watch you chew your food, and even read your license plate when you get in your car! Why? The Bible creates the presence of God and forces a reaction in people's hearts.

3. *The Nature Of A Person Is Changed When He Or She Reads The Bible.* People change. Peace enters into their spirits. Joy wells up within their lives.

People like what they become when they read this book. They accept Christ because this Bible says Jesus Christ is the Son of God and that all have sinned and the wages of sin will bring death; and the only forgiveness they can find is through Jesus, the Son of God.

3 Basic Reasons For Accepting Christ

1. *You Need Forgiveness.* At some point in your life, you will want to be clean. You will hate guilt; you will crave purity. You have a built-in desire toward God, and you will have to address that appetite at some point in your life.

2. *You Need A Friend.* You may be sitting there saying, "But, don't I have friends." Yes, but you have never had a friend like Jesus. Nobody can handle the information about your life as well as He can. He is the most consistent relationship you will ever know. Human friends vacillate in their reaction, depending on your mood or theirs. Jesus Christ never changes His opinion of you. Nobody can tell Him anything which will change His mind about you. You cannot enjoy His world without His companionship.

3. *You Need A Future.* All men have a built-in need for immortality, a craving for an eternity. God placed it within us. D.L. Moody once made a statement, "One of these days you are going to hear that I'm dead and gone. When you do, don't believe a word of it. I'll be more alive then, than at any other time in my life." Each of us wonders about eternity. What is death like? What happens when I die? Is there a hell? a heaven? a God? a devil? What happens? Every man wants to be around tomorrow. The only guarantee you will have of a future is to have the Eternal One on the inside of you. *He is Jesus Christ, the Son of God!*

The Gospel means Good News. You can change. Your sins can be forgiven. Your guilt can be dissolved. God loves *you!* He wants to be the difference in your life. "All have sinned, and come short of the glory of God" (Romans 3:23). "The wages of sin is death" (Romans 6:23).

What does that mean? First, it means that all unconfessed sin will be judged and penalized. But that is not the end of the story. The second part of verse 23 says, "but the gift of God is eternal life through Jesus Christ our Lord." This means that between the wrath and judgment of God upon your sin, Jesus Christ the Son of God stepped in and absorbed your judgment and your penalty for you. God says if you recognize and respect Him and His worth as the Son of God, judgment will be withheld, and you will receive a pardon, forgiveness of every past sin.

What should you do? "If you believe in your heart that Jesus is the Son of God and that God raised Him from the dead on the third day, and confess that with your mouth, then you will be saved" (Romans 10:9,10). "Saved" means *removed from danger.* It simply means if you accept Jesus Christ, God will take you out of the danger zone and receive you as a child of the Most High God.

What is His gift that you are to receive? His Son. "For God so loved the world, that He gave His only begotten Son, that whosoever believeth in Him should not perish, but have everlasting life" (John 3:16).

How do you accept His Son? Accept His mercy.

How do you reject your sins? Confess them and turn away from them. "If I confess my sins He is faithful and just to forgive me my sins and to cleanse me from all unrighteousness" (1 John 1:9).

This is the Gospel.

Your Business Decisions

1

When You Are Asked To Participate In Unscrupulous Business Activities

Ye shall do no unrighteousness in judgment, in meteyard, in weight, or in measure. *Leviticus 19:35*

Just balances, just weights, a just ephah, and a just hin, shall ye have: I am the Lord your God, which brought you out of the land of Egypt. *Leviticus 19:36*

But thou shalt have a perfect and just weight, a perfect and just measure shalt thou have: that thy days may be lengthened in the land which the Lord thy God giveth thee. *Deuteronomy 25:15*

He that hath clean hands, and a pure heart; who hath not lifted up his soul unto vanity, nor sworn deceitfully. *Psalm 24:4*

A false balance is abomination to the Lord: but a just weight is His delight.
Proverbs 11:1

The integrity of the upright shall guide them: but the perverseness of transgressors shall destroy them. *Proverbs 11:3*

Lying lips are abomination to the Lord: but they that deal truly are His delight.
Proverbs 12:22

He that walketh righteously, and speaketh uprightly; he that despiseth the gain of oppressions, that shaketh his hands from holding of bribes, that stoppeth his ears from hearing of blood, and shutteth his eyes from seeing evil;

He shall dwell on high: his place of defence shall be the munitions of rocks: bread shall be given him; his waters shall be sure. *Isaiah 33:15,16*

And he said unto them, Exact no more

than that which is appointed you.
Luke 3:13

And as ye would that men should do to you, do ye also to them likewise. *Luke 6:31*

And herein do I exercise myself, to have always a conscience void of offence toward God, and toward men. *Acts 24:16*

But have renounced the hidden things of dishonesty, not walking in craftiness, nor handling the word of God deceitfully; but by manifestation of the truth commending ourselves to every man's conscience in the sight of God. *2 Corinthians 4:2*

Receive us; we have wronged no man, we have corrupted no man, we have defrauded no man. *2 Corinthians 7:2*

Providing for honest things, not only in the sight of the Lord, but also in the sight of men. *2 Corinthians 8:21*

Pray for us: for we trust we have a good conscience, in all things willing to live honestly. *Hebrews 13:18*

Your Ability To Listen
Creates
The Rewards Of Change.

-MIKE MURDOCK

Copyright © 2001 by Mike Murdock • Wisdom International
The Wisdom Center • P.O. Box 99 • Denton, TX 76202

2

WHEN YOU FACE UNFAIR COMPLAINTS OR CRITICISM

Trust in the Lord, and do good; so shalt thou dwell in the land, and verily thou shalt be fed. *Psalm 37:3*

Delight thyself also in the Lord; and He shall give thee the desires of thine heart.
Psalm 37:4

Commit thy way unto the Lord; trust also in Him; and He shall bring it to pass.
Psalm 37:5

And He shall bring forth thy righteousness as the light, and thy judgment as the noonday. *Psalm 37:6*

For evildoers shall be cut off: but those that wait upon the Lord, they shall inherit the earth. *Psalm 37:9*

The discretion of a man deferreth his anger; and it is his glory to pass over a transgression. *Proverbs 19:11*

He that hath no rule over his own spirit is like a city that is broken down, and without walls. *Proverbs 25:28*

Better is the end of a thing than the beginning thereof: and the patient in spirit is better than the proud in spirit.
Ecclesiastes 7:8

Be not hasty in thy spirit to be angry: for anger resteth in the bosom of fools.
Ecclesiastes 7:9

And as ye would that men should do to you, do ye also to them likewise. *Luke 6:31*

In your patience possess ye your souls.
Luke 21:19

Be careful for nothing; but in every thing by prayer and supplication with thanksgiving let your requests be made known unto God. *Philippians 4:6*

And that ye study to be quiet, and to do your own business, and to work with your own hands, as we commanded you;
1 Thessalonians 4:11

That ye may walk honestly toward them that are without, and that ye may have lack of nothing. *1 Thessalonians 4:12*

And the servant of the Lord must not strive; but be gentle unto all men, apt to teach, patient, *2 Timothy 2:24*

Knowing this, that the trying of your faith worketh patience. *James 1:3*

But let patience have her perfect work, that ye may be perfect and entire, wanting nothing. *James 1:4*

Wherefore, my beloved brethren, let every man be swift to hear, slow to speak, slow to wrath: *James 1:19*

For this is thankworthy, if a man for conscience toward God endure grief, suffering wrongfully. *1 Peter 2:19*

The Only Reason Men Fail Is Broken Focus.

-MIKE MURDOCK

Copyright © 2001 by Mike Murdock • Wisdom International
The Wisdom Center • P.O. Box 99 • Denton, TX 76202

3

WHEN YOUR BUSINESS IS FAILING

But if from thence thou shalt seek the Lord thy God, thou shalt find Him, if thou seek Him with all thy heart and with all thy soul.
Deuteronomy 4:29

When thou art in tribulation, and all these things are come upon thee, even in the latter days, if thou turn to the Lord thy God, and shalt be obedient unto His voice;
Deuteronomy 4:30

Be strong and of a good courage, fear not, nor be afraid of them: for the Lord thy God, He it is that doth go with thee; He will not fail thee, nor forsake thee.
Deuteronomy 31:6

This book of the law shall not depart out of thy mouth; but thou shalt meditate therein day and night, that thou mayest observe to do according to all that is written therein: for then thou shalt make thy way prosperous, and then thou shalt have good success. *Joshua 1:8*

Have I not commanded thee? Be strong and of a good courage; be not afraid, neither be thou dismayed: for the Lord thy God is with thee whithersoever thou goest.
Joshua 1:9

And David said to Solomon his son, Be strong and of good courage, and do it: fear not, nor be dismayed: for the Lord God, even my God, will be with thee; He will not fail thee, nor forsake thee, until thou hast finished all the work for the service of the house of the Lord. *1 Chronicles 28:20*

Teach me Thy way, O Lord, and lead me in a plain path, because of mine enemies.
Psalm 27:11

For Thou art my rock and my fortress; therefore for Thy name's sake lead me, and guide me. *Psalm 31:3*

What time I am afraid, I will trust in Thee. *Psalm 56:3*

In God I will praise His word, in God I have put my trust; I will not fear what flesh can do unto me. *Psalm 56:4*

He shall not be afraid of evil tidings: his heart is fixed, trusting in the Lord.
Psalm 112:7

It is better to trust in the Lord than to put confidence in man. *Psalm 118:8*

Trust in the Lord with all thine heart; and lean not unto thine own understanding.
Proverbs 3:5

The name of the Lord is a strong tower: the righteous runneth into it, and is safe.
Proverbs 18:10

Nay, in all these things we are more than conquerors through Him that loved us.
Romans 8:37

I can do all things through Christ which strengtheneth me. *Philippians 4:13*

Those Without Your Pain Will Never Understand Your Passion.

-MIKE MURDOCK

Copyright © 2001 by Mike Murdock • Wisdom International
The Wisdom Center • P.O. Box 99 • Denton, TX 76202

4

WHEN YOU FACE A HOSTILE BOARD

I said, I will take heed to my ways, that I sin not with my tongue: I will keep my mouth with a bridle, while the wicked is before me. *Psalm 39:1*

Whoso offereth praise glorifieth Me: and to him that ordereth his conversation aright will I shew the salvation of God.
Psalm 50:23

Set a watch, O Lord, before my mouth; keep the door of my lips. *Psalm 141:3*

The mouth of a righteous man is a well of life: *Proverbs 10:11*

There is that speaketh like the piercings of a sword: but the tongue of the wise is health. *Proverbs 12:18*

The lip of truth shall be established for

ever: but a lying tongue is but for a moment.
Proverbs 12:19

Pleasant words are as an honeycomb, sweet to the soul, and health to the bones.
Proverbs 16:24

He that hath knowledge spareth his words: and a man of understanding is of an excellent spirit. *Proverbs 17:27*

Even a fool, when he holdeth his peace, is counted wise: and he that shutteth his lips is esteemed a man of understanding.
Proverbs 17:28

Whoso keepeth his mouth and his tongue keepeth his soul from troubles.
Proverbs 21:23

For by thy words thou shalt be justified, and by thy words thou shalt be condemned.
Matthew 12:37

A good man out of the good treasure of his heart bringeth forth that which is good; and an evil man out of the evil treasure of his heart bringeth forth that which is evil: for of the abundance of the heart his mouth speaketh. *Luke 6:45*

Let no corrupt communication proceed out of your mouth, but that which is good to the use of edifying, that it may minister grace unto the hearers. *Ephesians 4:29*

Let your speech be alway with grace, seasoned with salt, that ye may know how ye ought to answer every man.
Colossians 4:6

Wherefore, my beloved brethren, let every man be swift to hear, slow to speak, slow to wrath: *James 1:19*

Who is a wise man endued with knowledge among you? let him shew out of a good conversation his works with meekness of wisdom. *James 3:13*

For where envying and strife is, there is confusion and every evil work.

But the wisdom that is from above is first pure, then peaceable, gentle, and easy to be entreated, full of mercy and good fruits, without partiality, and without hypocrisy.

And the fruit of righteousness is sown in peace of them that make peace.
James 3:16-18

Nothing Is Ever As Bad As It First Appears.

-MIKE MURDOCK

Copyright © 2001 by Mike Murdock • Wisdom International
The Wisdom Center • P.O. Box 99 • Denton, TX 76202

5

WHEN A BUSINESS DEAL FALLS THROUGH

The Lord killeth, and maketh alive: He bringeth down to the grave, and bringeth up.
1 Samuel 2:6

The Lord maketh poor, and maketh rich: He bringeth low, and lifteth up.
1 Samuel 2:7

He will keep the feet of His saints, and the wicked shall be silent in darkness; for by strength shall no man prevail.
1 Samuel 2:9

For there is hope of a tree, if it be cut down, that it will sprout again, and that the tender branch thereof will not cease.
Job 14:7

Though the root thereof wax old in the earth, and the stock thereof die in the ground;
Job 14:8

For the needy shall not alway be forgotten: the expectation of the poor shall not perish for ever. *Psalm 9:18*

I will be glad and rejoice in Thy mercy: for Thou hast considered my trouble; Thou hast known my soul in adversities;
Psalm 31:7

Why art thou cast down, O my soul? and why art thou disquieted within me? hope in God: for I shall yet praise Him, who is the health of my countenance, and my God.
Psalm 43:5

I will meditate also of all Thy work, and talk of Thy doings. *Psalm 77:12*

Thou art the God that doest wonders: Thou hast declared Thy strength among the people. *Psalm 77:14*

The blessing of the Lord, it maketh rich, and He addeth no sorrow with it.
Proverbs 10:22

For surely there is an end; and thine expectation shall not be cut off.
Proverbs 23:18

If thou faint in the day of adversity, thy strength is small. *Proverbs 24:10*

Finally, my brethren, be strong in the Lord, and in the power of His might.
Ephesians 6:10

I know both how to be abased, and I know how to abound: every where and in all things I am instructed both to be full and to be hungry, both to abound and to suffer need. *Philippians 4:12*

I can do all things through Christ which strengtheneth me. *Philippians 4:13*

Let us therefore come boldly unto the throne of grace, that we may obtain mercy, and find grace to help in time of need.
Hebrews 4:16

When Wrong People
Leave Your Life,
Right Things
Start Happening.

-MIKE MURDOCK

Copyright © 2001 by Mike Murdock • Wisdom International
The Wisdom Center • P.O. Box 99 • Denton, TX 76202

6

WHEN YOUR PARTNERSHIP IS THREATENED

Lead me in Thy truth, and teach me: for Thou art the God of my salvation; on Thee do I wait all the day. *Psalm 25:5*

Mine eyes are ever toward the Lord; for He shall pluck my feet out of the net.
Psalm 25:15

Thy God hath commanded thy strength: strengthen, O God, that which Thou hast wrought for us. *Psalm 68:28*

Order my steps in Thy word: and let not any iniquity have dominion over me.
Psalm 119:133

Strive not with a man without cause, if he have done thee no harm. *Proverbs 3:30*

Only by pride cometh contention: but

with the well advised is wisdom.
Proverbs 13:10

A wrathful man stirreth up strife: but he that is slow to anger appeaseth strife.
Proverbs 15:18

A froward man soweth strife: and a whisperer separateth chief friends.
Proverbs 16:28

Cast out the scorner, and contention shall go out; yea, strife and reproach shall cease.
Proverbs 22:10

But they that wait upon the Lord shall renew their strength; they shall mount up with wings as eagles; they shall run, and not be weary; and they shall walk, and not faint.
Isaiah 40:31

Fear thou not; for I am with thee: be not dismayed; for I am thy God: I will strengthen thee; yea, I will help thee; yea, I will uphold thee with the right hand of my righteousness.
Isaiah 41:10

Behold, all they that were incensed

against thee shall be ashamed and confounded: they shall be as nothing; and they that strive with thee shall perish.
Isaiah 41:11

Blessed are the peacemakers: for they shall be called the children of God.
Matthew 5:9

Moreover if thy brother shall trespass against thee, go and tell him his fault between thee and him alone: if he shall hear thee, thou hast gained thy brother.
Matthew 18:15

If it be possible, as much as lieth in you, live peaceably with all men.   *Romans 12:18*

Let us therefore follow after the things which make for peace, and things wherewith one may edify another.   *Romans 14:19*

For to one is given by the Spirit the word of wisdom; to another the word of knowledge by the same Spirit;   *1 Corinthians 12:8*

But without faith it is impossible to please Him; for he that cometh to God must

believe that He is, and that He is a rewarder of them that diligently seek Him.
Hebrews 11:6

If any of you lack wisdom, let him ask of God, that giveth to all men liberally, and upbraideth not; and it shall be given him.
James 1:5

For where envying and strife is, there is confusion and every evil work.
James 3:16

But the wisdom that is from above is first pure, then peaceable, gentle, and easy to be entreated, full of mercy and good fruits, without partiality, and without hypocrisy.
James 3:17

And the fruit of righteousness is sown in peace of them that make peace.
James 3:18

7

WHEN YOU WANT TO CHANGE YOUR PROFESSION

And He said, My presence shall go with thee, and I will give thee rest. *Exodus 33:14*

He found him in a desert land, and in the waste howling wilderness; He led him about, He instructed him, He kept him as the apple of his eye. *Deuteronomy 32:10*

For Thou art my lamp, O Lord: and the Lord will lighten my darkness.
2 Samuel 22:29

Thou gavest also Thy good spirit to instruct them, and withheldest not thy manna from their mouth, and gavest them water for their thirst. *Nehemiah 9:20*

Lead me, O Lord, in Thy righteousness because of mine enemies; make Thy way straight before my face. *Psalm 5:8*

He maketh me to lie down in green pastures: He leadeth me beside the still waters. *Psalm 23:2*

He restoreth my soul: He leadeth me in the paths of righteousness for His name's sake. *Psalm 23:3*

Teach me Thy way, O Lord, and lead me in a plain path, because of mine enemies.
Psalm 27:11

For Thou art my rock and my fortress; therefore for Thy name's sake lead me, and guide me. *Psalm 31:3*

I will instruct thee and teach thee in the way which thou shalt go: I will guide thee with Mine eye. *Psalm 32:8*

For this God is our God for ever and ever: He will be our guide even unto death.
Psalm 48:14

Thou shalt guide me with thy counsel, and afterward receive me to glory.
Psalm 73:24

Even there shall Thy hand lead me, and Thy right hand shall hold me. *Psalm 139:10*

I lead in the way of righteousness, in the midst of the paths of judgment:
Proverbs 8:20

He shall feed His flock like a shepherd: He shall gather the lambs with His arm, and carry them in His bosom, and shall gently lead those that are with young.
Isaiah 40:11

And I will bring the blind by a way that they knew not; I will lead them in paths that they have not known: I will make darkness light before them, and crooked things straight. These things will I do unto them, and not forsake them. *Isaiah 42:16*

Thus saith the Lord, thy Redeemer, the Holy One of Israel; I am the Lord thy God which teacheth thee to profit, which leadeth thee by the way that thou shouldest go.
Isaiah 48:17

And the Lord shall guide thee continually, and satisfy thy soul in drought, and make fat thy bones: and thou shalt be like a watered garden, and like a spring of water, whose waters fail not. *Isaiah 58:11*

Howbeit when He, the Spirit of truth, is come, He will guide you into all truth: for He shall not speak of Himself; but whatsoever He shall hear, that shall He speak: and He will shew you things to come.
John 16:13

~ 8 ~

WHEN YOU START A NEW BUSINESS

The meek will He guide in judgment: and the meek will He teach His way.
Psalm 25:9

For Thou art my rock and my fortress; therefore for Thy name's sake lead me, and guide me.
Psalm 31:3

I will instruct thee and teach thee in the way which thou shalt go: I will guide thee with Mine eye.
Psalm 32:8

Thou shalt guide me with Thy counsel, and afterward receive me to glory.
Psalm 73:24

A good man sheweth favour, and lendeth: he will guide his affairs with discretion.
Psalm 112:5

For the Lord giveth wisdom: out of His

mouth cometh knowledge and understanding. *Proverbs 2:6*

Trust in the Lord with all thine heart; and lean not unto thine own understanding. *Proverbs 3:5*

He becometh poor that dealeth with a slack hand: but the hand of the diligent maketh rich. *Proverbs 10:4*

The hand of the diligent shall bear rule: but the slothful shall be under tribute. *Proverbs 12:24*

The soul of the sluggard desireth, and hath nothing: but the soul of the diligent shall be made fat. *Proverbs 13:4*

Without counsel purposes are disappointed: but in the multitude of counsellors they are established. *Proverbs 15:22*

Love not sleep, lest thou come to poverty; open thine eyes, and thou shalt be satisfied with bread. *Proverbs 20:13*

Seest thou a man diligent in his business? he shall stand before kings; he

shall not stand before mean men.
Proverbs 22:29

Through wisdom is an house builded; and by understanding it is established:
Proverbs 24:3

He that tilleth his land shall have plenty of bread: but he that followeth after vain persons shall have poverty enough.
Proverbs 28:19

In the morning sow thy seed, and in the evening withhold not thine hand: for thou knowest not whether shall prosper, either this or that, or whether they both shall be alike good. *Ecclesiastes 11:6*

Fear thou not; for I am with thee: be not dismayed; for I am thy God: I will strengthen thee; yea, I will help thee; yea, I will uphold thee with the right hand of My righteousness. *Isaiah 41:10*

But seek ye first the kingdom of God, and His righteousness; and all these things shall be added unto you. *Matthew 6:33*

Not slothful in business; fervent in spirit; serving the Lord; *Romans 12:11*

9

WHEN YOUR COMPETITOR HAS AN ADVANTAGE OVER YOU

Seek the Lord and His strength, seek His face continually. *1 Chronicles 16:11*

The righteous also shall hold on his way, and he that hath clean hands shall be stronger and stronger. *Job 17:9*

For the Lord loveth judgment, and forsaketh not His saints; they are preserved for ever: but the seed of the wicked shall be cut off. *Psalm 37:28*

Thou shalt guide me with Thy counsel, and afterward receive me to glory. *Psalm 73:24*

But the path of the just is as the shining light, that shineth more and more unto the perfect day. *Proverbs 4:18*

But he that shall endure unto the end, the same shall be saved. *Matthew 24:13*

But I have prayed for thee, that thy faith fail not: and when thou art converted, strengthen thy brethren. *Luke 22:32*

Abide in Me, and I in you. As the branch cannot bear fruit of itself, except it abide in the vine; no more can ye, except ye abide in Me. *John 15:4*

I am the vine, ye are the branches: He that abideth in Me, and I in him, the same bringeth forth much fruit: for without me ye can do nothing. *John 15:5*

If ye abide in Me, and My words abide in you, ye shall ask what ye will, and it shall be done unto you. *John 15:7*

Nay, in all these things we are more than conquerors through Him that loved us. *Romans 8:37*

For I am persuaded, that neither death, nor life, nor angels, nor principalities, nor powers, nor things present, nor things to come, *Romans 8:38*

Nor height, nor depth, nor any other creature, shall be able to separate us from the love of God, which is in Christ Jesus our Lord. *Romans 8:39*

Therefore, my beloved brethren, be ye stedfast, unmoveable, always abounding in the work of the Lord, forasmuch as ye know that your labour is not in vain in the Lord.
1 Corinthians 15:58

Watch ye, stand fast in the faith, quit you like men, be strong. *1 Corinthians 16:13*

Wherefore take unto you the whole armour of God, that ye may be able to withstand in the evil day, and having done all, to stand. *Ephesians 6:13*

Being confident of this very thing, that He which hath begun a good work in you will perform it until the day of Jesus Christ:
Philippians 1:6

Therefore, my brethren dearly beloved and longed for, my joy and crown, so stand fast in the Lord, my dearly beloved.
Philippians 4:1

Wherefore seeing we also are compassed about with so great a cloud of witnesses, let us lay aside every weight, and the sin which doth so easily beset us, and let us run with patience the race that is set before us, *Hebrews 12:1*

Looking unto Jesus the author and finisher of our faith; who for the joy that was set before Him endured the cross, despising the shame, and is set down at the right hand of the throne of God. *Hebrews 12:2*

Casting all your care upon Him; for He careth for you. *1 Peter 5:7*

Be sober, be vigilant; because your adversary the devil, as a roaring lion, walketh about, seeking whom he may devour: *1 Peter 5:8*

Whom resist stedfast in the faith, knowing that the same afflictions are accomplished in your brethren that are in the world. *1 Peter 5:9*

Your Customers

≈ 10 ≈

When A Customer Is Dissatisfied

Cease from anger, and forsake wrath: fret not thyself in any wise to do evil.
Psalm 37:8

A soft answer turneth away wrath: but grievous words stir up anger. *Proverbs 15:1*

A wrathful man stirreth up strife: but he that is slow to anger appeaseth strife.
Proverbs 15:18

Better is the end of a thing than the beginning thereof: and the patient in spirit is better than the proud in spirit.
Ecclesiastes 7:8

In your patience possess ye your souls.
Luke 21:19

Charity suffereth long, and is kind; charity envieth not; charity vaunteth not itself, is not puffed up, *1 Corinthians 13:4*

Doth not behave itself unseemly, seeketh not her own, is not easily provoked, thinketh no evil; *1 Corinthians 13:5*

But in all things approving ourselves as the ministers of God, in much patience, in afflictions, in necessities, in distresses, *2 Corinthians 6:4*

By pureness, by knowledge, by longsuffering, by kindness, by the Holy Ghost, by love unfeigned, *2 Corinthians 6:6*

That ye might walk worthy of the Lord unto all pleasing, being fruitful in every good work, and increasing in the knowledge of God; *Colossians 1:10*

Strengthened with all might, according to His glorious power, unto all patience and longsuffering with joyfulness;

Colossians 1:11

Put on therefore, as the elect of God, holy and beloved, bowels of mercies, kindness, humbleness of mind, meekness, longsuffering; *Colossians 3:12*

Forbearing one another, and forgiving one another, if any man have a quarrel against any: even as Christ forgave you, so also do ye. *Colossians 3:13*

Now we exhort you, brethren, warn them that are unruly, comfort the feebleminded, support the weak, be patient toward all men. *1 Thessalonians 5:14*

But thou, O man of God, flee these things; and follow after righteousness, godliness, faith, love, patience, meekness.
1 Timothy 6:11

For ye have need of patience, that, after ye have done the will of God, ye might receive the promise. *Hebrews 10:36*

Be patient therefore, brethren, unto the coming of the Lord. Behold, the husbandman waiteth for the precious fruit of the earth, and hath long patience for it, until he receive the early and latter rain. *James 5:7*

Be ye also patient; stablish your hearts: for the coming of the Lord draweth nigh.
James 5:8

11

WHEN A CUSTOMER OFFENDS YOU

I said, I will take heed to my ways, that I sin not with my tongue: I will keep my mouth with a bridle, while the wicked is before me.
Psalm 39:1

The lip of truth shall be established for ever: but a lying tongue is but for a moment.
Proverbs 12:19

Whoso keepeth his mouth and his tongue keepeth his soul from troubles.
Proverbs 21:23

Answer not a fool according to his folly, lest thou also be like unto him.
Proverbs 26:4

But I say unto you, That ye resist not evil: but whosoever shall smite thee on thy right cheek, turn to him the other also.
Matthew 5:39

Give to him that asketh thee, and from him that would borrow of thee turn not thou away. *Matthew 5:42*

Recompense to no man evil for evil. Provide things honest in the sight of all men. *Romans 12:17*

If it be possible, as much as lieth in you, live peaceably with all men. *Romans 12:18*

Dearly beloved, avenge not yourselves, but rather give place unto wrath: for it is written, Vengeance is Mine; I will repay, saith the Lord. *Romans 12:19*

Be not overcome of evil, but overcome evil with good. *Romans 12:21*

See that none render evil for evil unto any man; but ever follow that which is good, both among yourselves, and to all men.
1 Thessalonians 5:15

Follow peace with all men, and holiness, without which no man shall see the Lord:
Hebrews 12:14

But the wisdom that is from above is first pure, then peaceable, gentle, and easy to be intreated, full of mercy and good fruits, without partiality, and without hypocrisy.
James 3:17

And the fruit of righteousness is sown in peace of them that make peace.
James 3:18

For this is thankworthy, if a man for conscience toward God endure grief, suffering wrongfully. *1 Peter 2:19*

For what glory is it, if, when ye be buffeted for your faults, ye shall take it patiently? but if, when ye do well, and suffer for it, ye take it patiently, this is acceptable with God. *1 Peter 2:20*

☙ 12 ❧

WHEN A CUSTOMER REFUSES TO PAY YOU

I will instruct thee and teach thee in the way which thou shalt go: I will guide thee with Mine eye. *Psalm 32:8*

Teach me good judgment and knowledge: for I have believed Thy commandments. *Psalm 119:66*

For the merchandise of it is better than the merchandise of silver, and the gain thereof than fine gold. *Proverbs 3:14*

For the Lord shall be thy confidence, and shall keep thy foot from being taken. *Proverbs 3:26*

Poverty and shame shall be to him that refuseth instruction: but he that regardeth reproof shall be honoured. *Proverbs 13:18*

Correction is grievous unto him that forsaketh the way: and he that hateth reproof shall die. *Proverbs 15:10*

A scorner loveth not one that reproveth him: neither will he go unto the wise.
Proverbs 15:12

A reproof entereth more into a wise man than an hundred stripes into a fool.
Proverbs 17:10

When the scorner is punished, the simple is made wise: and when the wise is instructed, he receiveth knowledge.
Proverbs 21:11

He that rebuketh a man afterwards shall find more favour than he that flattereth with the tongue. *Proverbs 28:23*

Moreover if thy brother shall trespass against thee, go and tell him his fault between thee and him alone: if he shall hear thee, thou hast gained thy brother.
Matthew 18:15

Take heed to yourselves: If thy brother

trespass against thee, rebuke him; and if he repent, forgive him. *Luke 17:3*

Doth not behave itself unseemly, seeketh not her own, is not easily provoked, thinketh no evil; *1 Corinthians 13:5*

Rejoiceth not in iniquity, but rejoiceth in the truth; *1 Corinthians 13:6*

Beareth all things, believeth all things, hopeth all things, endureth all things. *1 Corinthians 13:7*

Now we exhort you, brethren, warn them that are unruly, comfort the feebleminded, support the weak, be patient toward all men. *1 Thessalonians 5:14*

If any of you lack wisdom, let him ask of God, that giveth to all men liberally, and upbraideth not; and it shall be given him. *James 1:5*

≈ 13 ≈

WHEN A CUSTOMER DECEIVES YOU

Thou preparest a table before me in the presence of mine enemies: Thou anointest my head with oil; my cup runneth over.
Psalm 23:5

For Thou art my rock and my fortress; therefore for Thy name's sake lead me, and guide me. *Psalm 31:3*

Pull me out of the net that they have laid privily for me: for Thou art my strength.
Psalm 31:4

Into Thine hand I commit my spirit: Thou hast redeemed me, O Lord God of truth. *Psalm 31:5*

Thou art my hiding place; Thou shalt preserve me from trouble; Thou shalt compass me about with songs of deliverance.
Psalm 32:7

Rest in the Lord, and wait patiently for Him: fret not thyself because of him who prospereth in his way, because of the man who bringeth wicked devices to pass.
Psalm 37:7

For in Thee, O Lord, do I hope: thou wilt hear, O Lord my God. *Psalm 38:15*

In my distress I cried unto the Lord, and He heard me. *Psalm 120:1*

Deliver my soul, O Lord, from lying lips, and from a deceitful tongue. *Psalm 120:2*

The lip of truth shall be established for ever: but a lying tongue is but for a moment.
Proverbs 12:19

Commit thy works unto the Lord, and thy thoughts shall be established.
Proverbs 16:3

Say not, I will do so to him as he hath done to me: I will render to the man according to his work. *Proverbs 24:29*

And the Lord shall guide thee continually, and satisfy thy soul in drought, and make fat thy bones: and thou shalt be like a watered garden, and like a spring of water, whose waters fail not.   *Isaiah 58:11*

I the Lord search the heart, I try the reins, even to give every man according to his ways, and according to the fruit of his doings.   *Jeremiah 17:10*

And when ye stand praying, forgive, if ye have aught against any: that your Father also which is in heaven may forgive you your trespasses.   *Mark 11:25*

But if ye do not forgive, neither will your Father which is in heaven forgive your trespasses.   *Mark 11:26*

And who is he that will harm you, if ye be followers of that which is good?
1 Peter 3:13

~ 14 ~

WHEN A CUSTOMER BECOMES A NUISANCE

He that is slow to wrath is of great understanding: but he that is hasty of spirit exalteth folly.   *Proverbs 14:29*

A soft answer turneth away wrath: but grievous words stir up anger.   *Proverbs 15:1*

He that is slow to anger is better than the mighty; and he that ruleth his spirit than he that taketh a city.   *Proverbs 16:32*

The discretion of a man deferreth his anger; and it is his glory to pass over a transgression.   *Proverbs 19:11*

It is an honour for a man to cease from strife: but every fool will be meddling.
   Proverbs 20:3

Better is the end of a thing than the

beginning thereof: and the patient in spirit is better than the proud in spirit.
Ecclesiastes 7:8

If the spirit of the ruler rise up against thee, leave not thy place; for yielding pacifieth great offences. *Ecclesiastes 10:4*

Blessed are the meek: for they shall inherit the earth. *Matthew 5:5*

Blessed are the peacemakers: for they shall be called the children of God.
Matthew 5:9

Bless them which persecute you: bless, and curse not. *Romans 12:14*

If it be possible, as much as lieth in you, live peaceably with all men. *Romans 12:18*

Beareth all things, believeth all things, hopeth all things, endureth all things.
1 Corinthians 13:7

Now we exhort you, brethren, warn them that are unruly, comfort the feebleminded, support the weak, be patient toward all men. *1 Thessalonians 5:14*

And the servant of the Lord must not strive; but be gentle unto all men, apt to teach, patient, *2 Timothy 2:24*

To speak evil of no man, to be no brawlers, but gentle, shewing all meekness unto all men. *Titus 3:2*

Follow peace with all men, and holiness, without which no man shall see the Lord: *Hebrews 12:14*

And the fruit of the righteousness is sown in peace of them that make peace. *James 3:18*

~ 15 ~

WHEN A CUSTOMER IS DISHONEST

Quicken me, O Lord, for Thy name's sake: for Thy righteousness' sake bring my soul out of trouble.   *Psalm 143:11*

Give instruction to a wise man, and he will be yet wiser: teach a just man, and he will increase in learning.   *Proverbs 9:9*

Open rebuke is better than secret love.
   Proverbs 27:5

But love ye your enemies, and do good, and lend, hoping for nothing again; and your reward shall be great, and ye shall be the children of the Highest: for He is kind unto the unthankful and to the evil.   *Luke 6:35*

There hath no temptation taken you but such as is common to man: but God is faithful, who will not suffer you to be tempted

above that ye are able; but will with the temptation also make a way to escape, that ye may be able to bear it.
1 Corinthians 10:13

That He would grant you, according to the riches of His glory, to be strengthened with might by His Spirit in the inner man;
Ephesians 3:16

Finally, my brethren, be strong in the Lord, and in the power of His might.
Ephesians 6:10

For I know that this shall turn to my salvation through your prayer, and the supply of the Spirit of Jesus Christ,
Philippians 1:19

I can do all things through Christ which strengtheneth me. *Philippians 4:13*

Put on therefore, as the elect of God, holy and beloved, bowels of mercies, kindness, humbleness of mind, meekness, longsuffering; *Colossians 3:12*

Forbearing one another, and forgiving one another, if any man have a quarrel against any: even as Christ forgave you, so also do ye. *Colossians 3:13*

And above all these things put on charity, which is the bond of perfectness.
Colossians 3:14

And whatsoever ye do in word or deed, do all in the name of the Lord Jesus, giving thanks to God and the Father by him.
Colossians 3:17

~ 16 ~

WHEN A CUSTOMER EMBARRASSES YOU

Keep me as the apple of the eye, hide me under the shadow of Thy wings,
Psalm 17:8

For in the time of trouble He shall hide me in His pavilion: in the secret of His tabernacle shall He hide me; He shall set me up upon a rock. *Psalm 27:5*

And now shall mine head be lifted up above mine enemies round about me: therefore will I offer in His tabernacle sacrifices of joy; I will sing, yea, I will sing praises unto the Lord. *Psalm 27:6*

Thou art my hiding place; Thou shalt preserve me from trouble; Thou shalt compass me about with songs of deliverance.
Psalm 32:7

Hide me from the secret counsel of the wicked; from the insurrection of the workers of iniquity: *Psalm 64:2*

Hide not Thy face from me in the day when I am in trouble; incline Thine ear unto me: in the day when I call answer me speedily. *Psalm 102:2*

Thou art my hiding place and my shield: I hope in Thy word. *Psalm 119:114*

Set a watch, O Lord, before my mouth; keep the door of my lips. *Psalm 141:3*

Deliver me, O Lord, from mine enemies: I flee unto Thee to hide me. *Psalm 143:9*

Teach me to do Thy will; for Thou art my God: Thy spirit is good; lead me into the land of uprightness. *Psalm 143:10*

Whoso keepeth his mouth and his tongue keepeth his soul from troubles.
Proverbs 21:23

A word fitly spoken is like apples of gold in pictures of silver. *Proverbs 25:11*

A time to rend, and a time to sew; a time to keep silence, and a time to speak;
Ecclesiastes 3:7

Come, my people, enter thou into thy chambers, and shut thy doors about thee: hide thyself as it were for a little moment, until the indignation be overpast.
Isaiah 26:20

For by thy words thou shalt be justified, and by thy words thou shalt be condemned.
Matthew 12:37

Bless them that curse you, and pray for them which despitefully use you. *Luke 6:28*

Let no corrupt communication proceed out of your mouth, but that which is good to the use of edifying, that it may minister grace unto the hearers. *Ephesians 4:29*

Let your speech be alway with grace, seasoned with salt, that ye may know how ye ought to answer every man. *Colossians 4:6*

Wherefore, my beloved brethren, let every man be swift to hear, slow to speak, slow to wrath: *James 1:19*

Your Ignorance Is The Only Weapon An Adversary Can Use Against You.

-MIKE MURDOCK

Copyright © 2001 by Mike Murdock • Wisdom International
The Wisdom Center • P.O. Box 99 • Denton, TX 76202

17

WHEN A CUSTOMER TAKES YOU TO COURT

For the oppression of the poor, for the sighing of the needy, now will I arise, saith the Lord; I will set him in safety from him that puffeth at him. *Psalm 12:5*

The Lord hear thee in the day of trouble; the name of the God of Jacob defend thee;
Psalm 20:1

Judge me, O God, and plead my cause against an ungodly nation: O deliver me from the deceitful and unjust man.
Psalm 43:1

Why art thou cast down, O my soul? and why art thou disquieted within me? hope in God: for I shall yet praise Him, Who is the health of my countenance, and my God.
Psalm 43:5

For, lo, they lie in wait for my soul: the mighty are gathered against me; not for my transgression, nor for my sin, O Lord.
Psalm 59:3

They run and prepare themselves without my fault: awake to help me, and behold. *Psalm 59:4*

But I will sing of Thy power; yea, I will sing aloud of Thy mercy in the morning: for Thou hast been my defence and refuge in the day of my trouble. *Psalm 59:16*

Who redeemeth thy life from destruction; Who crowneth thee with lovingkindness and tender mercies;
Psalm 103:4

Trust in the Lord with all thine heart; and lean not unto thine own understanding.
Proverbs 3:5

In all thy ways acknowledge Him, and He shall direct thy paths. *Proverbs 3:6*

He that justifieth the wicked, and he that condemneth the just, even they both are abomination to the Lord.   *Proverbs 17:15*

Many seek the ruler's favour; but every man's judgment cometh from the Lord.
Proverbs 29:26

Blessed are ye, when men shall revile you, and persecute you, and shall say all manner of evil against you falsely, for My sake.   *Matthew 5:11*

And now, Lord, behold their threatenings: and grant unto Thy servants, that with all boldness they may speak Thy word,   *Acts 4:29*

Submit yourselves to every ordinance of man for the Lord's sake: whether it be to the king, as supreme;   *1 Peter 2:13*

For so is the will of God, that with well doing ye may put to silence the ignorance of foolish men: *1 Peter 2:15*

Having a good conscience; that, whereas they speak evil of you, as of evildoers, they may be ashamed that falsely accuse your good conversation in Christ.   *1 Peter 3:16*

Recognition
 Of Disorder
Is The First Step
 Toward Order.

-MIKE MURDOCK

Copyright © 2001 by Mike Murdock • Wisdom International
The Wisdom Center • P.O. Box 99 • Denton, TX 76202

Your Daily Schedule

~ 18 ~

When You Feel Disorganized

Shew me Thy ways, O Lord; teach me Thy paths. *Psalm 25:4*

The angel of the Lord encampeth round about them that fear Him, and delivereth them. *Psalm 34:7*

Behold, as the eyes of servants look unto the hand of their masters, and as the eyes of a maiden unto the hand of her mistress; so our eyes wait upon the Lord our God, until that He have mercy upon us. *Psalm 123:2*

Ponder the path of thy feet, and let all thy ways be established. *Proverbs 4:26*

Turn not to the right hand nor to the left: remove thy foot from evil.
Proverbs 4:27

A man's heart deviseth his way: but the Lord directeth his steps. *Proverbs 16:9*

If the iron be blunt, and he do not whet the edge, then must he put to more strength: but wisdom is profitable to direct.
Ecclesiastes 10:10

For the Lord God will help me; therefore shall I not be confounded: therefore have I set my face like a flint, and I know that I shall not be ashamed. *Isaiah 50:7*

O Lord, I know that the way of man is not in himself: it is not in man that walketh to direct his steps. *Jeremiah 10:23*

The Lord is good unto them that wait for Him, to the soul that seeketh Him.
Lamentations 3:25

And He said unto them, Come ye yourselves apart into a desert place, and rest a while: for there were many coming and going, and they had no leisure so much as to eat. *Mark 6:31*

Therefore, my beloved brethren, be ye stedfast, unmoveable, always abounding in the work of the Lord, forasmuch as ye know that your labour is not in vain in the Lord.
1 Corinthians 15:58

Watch ye, stand fast in the faith, quit you like men, be strong.
1 Corinthians 16:13

But ye, brethren, be not weary in well doing. *2 Thessalonians 3:13*

If any of you lack wisdom, let him ask of God, that giveth to all men liberally, and upbraideth not; and it shall be given him.
James 1:5

Wherefore gird up the loins of your mind, be sober, and hope to the end for the grace that is to be brought unto you at the revelation of Jesus Christ; *1 Peter 1:13*

Be sober, be vigilant; because your adversary the devil, as a roaring lion, walketh about, seeking whom he may devour: *1 Peter 5:8*

19

WHEN YOUR DAY FALLS APART

Cast me not away from Thy presence; and take not Thy Holy Spirit from me.
Psalm 51:11

Restore unto me the joy of Thy salvation; and uphold me with Thy free spirit.   *Psalm 51:12*

And the spirit of the Lord shall rest upon him, the spirit of wisdom and understanding, the spirit of counsel and might, the spirit of knowledge and of the fear of the Lord;   *Isaiah 11:2*

For I will pour water upon him that is thirsty, and floods upon the dry ground: I will pour My spirit upon thy seed, and My blessing upon thine offspring: *Isaiah 44:3*

And they shall spring up as among the grass, as willows by water courses. *Isaiah 44:4*

I, even I, am He that comforteth you: who art thou, that thou shouldest be afraid of a man that shall die, and of the son of man which shall be made as grass; *Isaiah 51:12*

So shall they fear the name of the Lord from the west, and His glory from the rising of the sun. When the enemy shall come in like a flood, the Spirit of the Lord shall lift up a standard against him. *Isaiah 59:19*

As for Me, this is My covenant with them, saith the Lord; My spirit that is upon thee, and My words which I have put in thy mouth, shall not depart out of thy mouth, nor out of the mouth of thy seed, nor out of the mouth of thy seed's seed, saith the Lord, from henceforth and for ever. *Isaiah 59:21*

But truly I am full of power by the spirit of the Lord, and of judgment, and of might, to declare unto Jacob his transgression, and to Israel his sin. *Micah 3:8*

But whosoever drinketh of the water that I shall give him shall never thirst; but the water that I shall give him shall be in him a well of water springing up into everlasting life. *John 4:14*

Even the Spirit of truth; Whom the world cannot receive, because it seeth Him not, neither knoweth Him: but ye know Him; for He dwelleth with you, and shall be in you.
John 14:17

But the Comforter, which is the Holy Ghost, Whom the Father will send in My name, He shall teach you all things, and bring all things to your remembrance, whatsoever I have said unto you.
John 14:26

Likewise the Spirit also helpeth our infirmities: for we know not what we should pray for as we ought: but the Spirit itself maketh intercession for us with groanings which cannot be uttered. *Romans 8:26*

And He that searcheth the hearts knoweth what is the mind of the Spirit, because He maketh intercession for the saints according to the will of God.
Romans 8:27

Who shall separate us from the love of Christ? shall tribulation, or distress, or persecution, or famine, or nakedness, or peril, or sword? *Romans 8:35*

Nay, in all these things we are more than conquerors through Him that loved us.
Romans 8:37

Now the God of hope fill you with all joy and peace in believing, that ye may abound in hope, through the power of the Holy Ghost. *Romans 15:13*

Finally, my brethren, be strong in the Lord, and in the power of His might.
Ephesians 6:10

Above all, taking the shield of faith, wherewith ye shall be able to quench all the fiery darts of the wicked. *Ephesians 6:16*

Praying always with all prayer and supplication in the Spirit, and watching thereunto with all perseverance and supplication for all saints; *Ephesians 6:18*

But ye, beloved, building up yourselves on your most holy faith, praying in the Holy Ghost, *Jude 1:20*

20

WHEN YOUR SCHEDULE IS OVERBOOKED

He maketh me to lie down in green pastures: He leadeth me beside the still waters. *Psalm 23:2*

He restoreth my soul: He leadeth me in the paths of righteousness for His name's sake. *Psalm 23:3*

Shew me Thy ways, O Lord; teach me Thy paths. *Psalm 25:4*

Lead me in Thy truth, and teach me: for Thou art the God of my salvation; on Thee do I wait all the day. *Psalm 25:5*

Let integrity and uprightness preserve me; for I wait on Thee. *Psalm 25:21*

Wait on the Lord: be of good courage, and He shall strengthen thine heart: wait, I say, on the Lord. *Psalm 27:14*

Rest in the Lord, and wait patiently for Him: fret not thyself because of him who prospereth in his way, because of the man who bringeth wicked devices to pass.
Psalm 37:7

The steps of a good man are ordered by the Lord: and he delighteth in His way.
Psalm 37:23

My soul waiteth for the Lord more than they that watch for the morning: I say, more than they that watch for the morning.
Psalm 130:6

Through wisdom is an house builded; and by understanding it is established:
Proverbs 24:3

Better is an handful with quietness, than both the hands full with travail and vexation of spirit. *Ecclesiastes 4:6*

Be not over much wicked, neither be thou foolish: why shouldest thou die before thy time? *Ecclesiastes 7:17*

For thus saith the Lord God, the Holy One of Israel; In returning and rest shall ye

be saved; in quietness and in confidence shall be your strength: and ye would not.
Isaiah 30:15

But they that wait upon the Lord shall renew their strength; they shall mount up with wings as eagles; they shall run, and not be weary; and they shall walk, and not faint.
Isaiah 40:31

And He said unto them, Come ye yourselves apart into a desert place, and rest a while: for there were many coming and going, and they had no leisure so much as to eat. *Mark 6:31*

And take heed to yourselves, lest at any time your hearts be overcharged with surfeiting, and drunkenness, and cares of this life, and so that day come upon you unawares. *Luke 21:34*

Wherefore seeing we also are compassed about with so great a cloud of witnesses, let us lay aside every weight, and the sin which doth so easily beset us, and let us run with patience the race that is set before us, *Hebrews 12:1*

21

WHEN YOU FACE CONSTANT INTERRUPTIONS

God is my strength and power: and He maketh my way perfect.   *2 Samuel 22:33*

He maketh my feet like hinds' feet: and setteth me upon my high places.
2 Samuel 22:34

The Lord is my rock, and my fortress, and my deliverer; my God, my strength, in whom I will trust; my buckler, and the horn of my salvation, and my high tower.
Psalm 18:2

With the merciful Thou wilt shew Thyself merciful; with an upright man Thou wilt shew Thyself upright;   *Psalm 18:25*

He that is slow to wrath is of great understanding: but he that is hasty of spirit exalteth folly.   *Proverbs 14:29*

He that is slow to anger is better than the mighty; and he that ruleth his spirit than he that taketh a city. *Proverbs 16:32*

Better is the end of a thing than the beginning thereof: and the patient in spirit is better than the proud in spirit.
Ecclesiastes 7:8

Be not hasty in thy spirit to be angry: for anger resteth in the bosom of fools.
Ecclesiastes 7:9

Give to him that asketh thee, and from him that would borrow of thee turn not thou away. *Matthew 5:42*

Take My yoke upon you, and learn of Me; for I am meek and lowly in heart: and ye shall find rest unto your souls.
Matthew 11:29

And let us not be weary in well doing: for in due season we shall reap, if we faint not. *Galatians 6:9*

Strengthened with all might, according to His glorious power, unto all patience and longsuffering with joyfulness; *Colossians 1:11*

Put on therefore, as the elect of God, holy and beloved, bowels of mercies, kindness, humbleness of mind, meekness, longsuffering; *Colossians 3:12*

Now we exhort you, brethren, warn them that are unruly, comfort the feebleminded, support the weak, be patient toward all men. *1 Thessalonians 5:14*

And the servant of the Lord must not strive; but be gentle unto all men, apt to teach, patient, *2 Timothy 2:24*

Knowing this, that the trying of your faith worketh patience. *James 1:3*

But let patience have her perfect work, that ye may be perfect and entire, wanting nothing. *James 1:4*

Wherefore, my beloved brethren, let every man be swift to hear, slow to speak, slow to wrath: *James 1:19*

~ 22 ~

WHEN YOU NEED A BREAK

Keep me as the apple of the eye, hide me under the shadow of Thy wings,
Psalm 17:8

He restoreth my soul: He leadeth me in the paths of righteousness for His name's sake. *Psalm 23:3*

For in the time of trouble He shall hide me in His pavilion: in the secret of His tabernacle shall He hide me; He shall set me up upon a rock. *Psalm 27:5*

Rest in the Lord, and wait patiently for Him: fret not thyself because of him who prospereth in his way, because of the man who bringeth wicked devices to pass.
Psalm 37:7

My heart panteth, my strength faileth me: as for the light of mine eyes, it also is gone from me. *Psalm 38:10*

For I am ready to halt, and my sorrow is continually before me. *Psalm 38:17*

Forsake me not, O Lord: O my God, be not far from me. *Psalm 38:21*

And I said, Oh that I had wings like a dove! for then would I fly away, and be at rest. *Psalm 55:6*

My flesh and my heart faileth: but God is the strength of my heart, and my portion for ever. *Psalm 73:26*

Return unto thy rest, O my soul; for the Lord hath dealt bountifully with thee.
Psalm 116:7

Quicken me, O Lord, for Thy name's sake: for Thy righteousness' sake bring my soul out of trouble. *Psalm 143:11*

Come, my people, enter thou into thy chambers, and shut thy doors about thee: hide thyself as it were for a little moment, until the indignation be overpast.
Isaiah 26:20

To whom He said, This is the rest

wherewith ye may cause the weary to rest; and this is the refreshing: yet they would not hear. *Isaiah 28:12*

And My people shall dwell in a peaceable habitation, and in sure dwellings, and in quiet resting places; *Isaiah 32:18*

Come unto Me, all ye that labour and are heavy laden, and I will give you rest.
Matthew 11:28

Take My yoke upon you, and learn of Me; for I am meek and lowly in heart: and ye shall find rest unto your souls.
Matthew 11:29

And He said unto them, Come ye yourselves apart into a desert place, and rest a while: for there were many coming and going, and they had no leisure so much as to eat. *Mark 6:31*

And they departed into a desert place by ship privately. *Mark 6:32*

There remaineth therefore a rest to the people of God. *Hebrews 4:9*

YOUR EMPLOYEES

~ 23 ~

WHEN YOUR EMPLOYEE DISAPPOINTS YOU

Thou shalt not avenge, nor bear any grudge against the children of thy people, but thou shalt love thy neighbour as thyself: I am the Lord.   *Leviticus 19:18*

O Lord my God, in Thee do I put my trust: save me from all them that persecute me, and deliver me: *Psalm 7:1*

Lest he tear my soul like a lion, rending it in pieces, while there is none to deliver.
Psalm 7:2

O my God, I trust in Thee: let me not be ashamed, let not mine enemies triumph over me.   *Psalm 25:2*

Trust in the Lord, and do good; so shalt thou dwell in the land, and verily thou shalt be fed. *Psalm 37:3*

Delight thyself also in the Lord; and He shall give thee the desires of thine heart.
Psalm 37:4

Commit thy way unto the Lord; trust also in Him; and He shall bring it to pass.
Psalm 37:5

And He shall bring forth thy righteousness as the light, and thy judgment as the noonday. *Psalm 37:6*

Cease from anger, and forsake wrath: fret not thyself in any wise to do evil.
Psalm 37:8

Say not thou, I will recompense evil; but wait on the Lord, and He shall save thee.
Proverbs 20:22

For My name's sake will I defer Mine anger, and for My praise will I refrain for thee, that I cut thee not off. *Isaiah 48:9*

For if ye forgive men their trespasses, your heavenly Father will also forgive you:
Matthew 6:14

And if he trespass against thee seven times in a day, and seven times in a day turn again to thee, saying, I repent; thou shalt forgive him. *Luke 17:4*

Recompense to no man evil for evil. Provide things honest in the sight of all men.
Romans 12:17

But we were gentle among you, even as a nurse cherisheth her children:
1 Thessalonians 2:7

And the servant of the Lord must not strive; but be gentle unto all men, apt to teach, patient, *2 Timothy 2:24*

And the Lord shall deliver me from every evil work, and will preserve me unto His heavenly kingdom: to Whom be glory for ever and ever. Amen. *2 Timothy 4:18*

To speak evil of no man, to be no brawlers, but gentle, shewing all meekness unto all men. *Titus 3:2*

24

WHEN YOUR EMPLOYEE CHEATS YOU

When the wicked, even mine enemies and my foes, came upon me to eat up my flesh, they stumbled and fell.   *Psalm 27:2*

I had fainted, unless I had believed to see the goodness of the Lord in the land of the living.   *Psalm 27:13*

Wait on the Lord: be of good courage, and He shall strengthen thine heart: wait, I say, on the Lord.   *Psalm 27:14*

The Lord is my strength and my shield; my heart trusted in Him, and I am helped: therefore my heart greatly rejoiceth; and with my song will I praise Him.   *Psalm 28:7*

Pull me out of the net that they have laid privily for me: for Thou art my strength.
Psalm 31:4

Make Thy face to shine upon Thy servant: save me for Thy mercies' sake.
Psalm 31:16

They rewarded me evil for good to the spoiling of my soul. *Psalm 35:12*

Yea, mine own familiar friend, in whom I trusted, which did eat of my bread, hath lifted up his heel against me. *Psalm 41:9*

But Thou, O Lord, be merciful unto me, and raise me up, that I may requite them.
Psalm 41:10

Cast thy burden upon the Lord, and He shall sustain thee: He shall never suffer the righteous to be moved. *Psalm 55:22*

What time I am afraid, I will trust in Thee. *Psalm 56:3*

In God have I put my trust: I will not be afraid what man can do unto me.
Psalm 56:11

But I will sing of Thy power; yea, I will sing aloud of Thy mercy in the morning: for Thou hast been my defence and refuge in the day of my trouble. *Psalm 59:16*

Unto Thee, O my strength, will I sing: for God is my defence, and the God of my mercy. *Psalm 59:17*

In Thee, O Lord, do I put my trust: let me never be put to confusion. *Psalm 71:1*

Let them be confounded and consumed that are adversaries to my soul; let them be covered with reproach and dishonour that seek my hurt. *Psalm 71:13*

My mouth shall shew forth Thy righteousness and Thy salvation all the day; for I know not the numbers thereof.
Psalm 71:15

I will go in the strength of the Lord God: I will make mention of Thy righteousness, even of Thine only. *Psalm 71:16*

Answer not a fool according to his folly, lest thou also be like unto him. *Proverbs 26:4*

Take heed to yourselves: If thy brother trespass against thee, rebuke him; and if he repent, forgive him. *Luke 17:3*

25

WHEN YOUR EMPLOYEE MAKES A COSTLY ERROR

He that covereth a transgression seeketh love; but he that repeateth a matter separateth very friends. *Proverbs 17:9*

A friend loveth at all times, and a brother is born for adversity. *Proverbs 17:17*

The discretion of a man deferreth his anger; and it is his glory to pass over a transgression. *Proverbs 19:11*

Ointment and perfume rejoice the heart: so doth the sweetness of a man's friend by hearty counsel. *Proverbs 27:9*

Blessed are the merciful: for they shall obtain mercy. *Matthew 5:7*

And forgive us our debts, as we forgive our debtors. *Matthew 6:12*

Recompense to no man evil for evil. Provide things honest in the sight of all men.
Romans 12:17

And be ye kind one to another, tenderhearted, forgiving one another, even as God for Christ's sake hath forgiven you.
Ephesians 4:32

Put on therefore, as the elect of God, holy and beloved, bowels of mercies, kindness, humbleness of mind, meekness, longsuffering; *Colossians 3:12*

Forbearing one another, and forgiving one another, if any man have a quarrel against any: even as Christ forgave you, so also do ye. *Colossians 3:13*

And above all these things put on charity, which is the bond of perfectness.
Colossians 3:14

And let us consider one another to provoke unto love and to good works:
Hebrews 10:24

Not rendering evil for evil, or railing for

railing: but contrariwise blessing; knowing that ye are thereunto called, that ye should inherit a blessing. *1 Peter 3:9*

And above all things have fervent charity among yourselves: for charity shall cover the multitude of sins. *1 Peter 4:8*

My little children, let us not love in word, neither in tongue; but in deed and in truth. *1 John 3:18*

26

WHEN YOUR EMPLOYEE SLANDERS YOU

He hath delivered my soul in peace from the battle that was against me: for there were many with me. *Psalm 55:18*

Cast thy burden upon the Lord, and He shall sustain thee: He shall never suffer the righteous to be moved. *Psalm 55:22*

Be merciful unto me, O God: for man would swallow me up; he fighting daily oppresseth me. *Psalm 56:1*

In God I will praise His word, in God I have put my trust; I will not fear what flesh can do unto me. *Psalm 56:4*

My soul is among lions: and I lie even among them that are set on fire, even the sons of men, whose teeth are spears and arrows, and their tongue a sharp sword.
Psalm 57:4

They have prepared a net for my steps; my soul is bowed down: they have digged a pit before me, into the midst whereof they are fallen themselves. Selah.   *Psalm 57:6*

Because of His strength will I wait upon Thee: for God is my defence.   *Psalm 59:9*

Whoso privily slandereth his neighbour, him will I cut off: him that hath a high look and a proud heart will not I suffer.
Psalm 101:5

He that hideth hatred with lying lips, and he that uttereth a slander, is a fool.
Proverbs 10:18

An hypocrite with his mouth destroyeth his neighbour: but through knowledge shall the just be delivered.   *Proverbs 11:9*

Let all bitterness, and wrath, and anger, and clamour, and evil speaking, be put away from you, with all malice: *Ephesians 4:31*

For he that will love life, and see good days, let him refrain his tongue from evil, and his lips that they speak no guile:
1 Peter 3:10

27

WHEN YOUR EMPLOYEE IS HURTING

Love ye therefore the stranger: for ye were strangers in the land of Egypt.
Deuteronomy 10:19

The Lord God hath given me the tongue of the learned, that I should know how to speak a word in season to him that is weary: he wakeneth morning by morning, he wakeneth mine ear to hear as the learned.
Isaiah 50:4

It is not to deal thy bread to the hungry, and that thou bring the poor that are cast out to thy house? when thou seest the naked, that thou cover him; and that thou hide not thyself from thine own flesh? *Isaiah 58:7*

Therefore all things whatsoever ye would that men should do to you, do ye even so to them: for this is the law and the prophets. *Matthew 7:12*

And the second is like unto it, Thou shalt love thy neighbour as thyself.
Matthew 22:39

Then shall the King say unto them on His right hand, Come, ye blessed of My Father, inherit the kingdom prepared for you from the foundation of the world:
For I was an hungered, and ye gave Me meat: I was thirsty, and ye gave Me drink: I was a stranger, and ye took Me in.
Naked, and ye clothed Me: I was sick, and ye visited Me: I was in prison, and ye came unto Me. *Matthew 25:34-36*

By this shall all men know that ye are My disciples, if ye have love one to another.
John 13:35

I have shewed you all things, how that so labouring ye ought to support the weak, and to remember the words of the Lord Jesus, how He said, It is more blessed to give than to receive. *Acts 20:35*

Rejoice with them that do rejoice, and weep with them that weep. *Romans 12:15*

We then that are strong ought to bear the infirmities of the weak, and not to please ourselves. *Romans 15:1*

Who comforteth us in all our tribulation, that we may be able to comfort them which are in any trouble, by the comfort wherewith we ourselves are comforted of God. *2 Corinthians 1:4*

Bear ye one another's burdens, and so fulfil the law of Christ. *Galatians 6:2*

Remember them that are in bonds, as bound with them; and them which suffer adversity, as being yourselves also in the body. *Hebrews 13:3*

But to do good and to communicate forget not: for with such sacrifices God is well pleased. *Hebrews 13:16*

If ye fulfil the royal law according to the scripture, Thou shalt love thy neighbour as thyself, ye do well: *James 2:8*

Finally, be ye all of one mind, having compassion one of another, love as brethren, be pitiful, be courteous: *1 Peter 3:8*

Your Reaction
 To Someone In Trouble
Determines God's Reaction
 To You The Next Time
You Get In Trouble.

-MIKE MURDOCK

Copyright © 2001 by Mike Murdock • Wisdom International
The Wisdom Center • P.O. Box 99 • Denton, TX 76202

28

WHEN YOUR EMPLOYEE HAS A PERSONAL CRISIS

Blessed is he that considereth the poor: the Lord will deliver him in time of trouble. *Psalm 41:1*

Withhold not good from them to whom it is due, when it is in the power of thine hand to do it. *Proverbs 3:27*

Say not unto thy neighbour, Go, and come again, and tomorrow I will give; when thou hast it by thee. *Proverbs 3:28*

Give to him that asketh thee, and from him that would borrow of thee turn not thou away. *Matthew 5:42*

And God is able to make all grace abound toward you; that ye, always having all sufficiency in all things, may abound to every good work: *2 Corinthians 9:8*

As it is written, He hath dispersed abroad; He hath given to the poor: His righteousness remaineth for ever.
2 Corinthians 9:9

Now He that ministereth seed to the sower both minister bread for your food, and multiply your seed sown, and increase the fruits of your righteousness;
2 Corinthians 9:10

Being enriched in every thing to all bountifulness, which causeth through us thanksgiving to God.   *2 Corinthians 9:11*

Brethren, if a man be overtaken in a fault, ye which are spiritual, restore such an one in the spirit of meekness; considering thyself, lest thou also be tempted.
Galatians 6:1

Bear ye one another's burdens, and so fulfil the law of Christ.   *Galatians 6:2*

For he that soweth to his flesh shall of the flesh reap corruption; but he that soweth to the Spirit shall of the Spirit reap life everlasting.   *Galatians 6:8*

As we have therefore opportunity, let us do good unto all men, especially unto them who are of the household of faith.
Galatians 6:10

But to do good and to communicate forget not: for with such sacrifices God is well pleased. *Hebrews 13:16*

If ye fulfil the royal law according to the scripture, Thou shalt love thy neighbour as thyself, ye do well: *James 2:8*

But if ye have respect to persons, ye commit sin, and are convinced of the law as transgressors. *James 2:9*

But whoso hath this world's good, and seeth his brother have need, and shutteth up his bowels of compassion from him, how dwelleth the love of God in him?
1 John 3:17

My little children, let us not love in word, neither in tongue; but in deed and in truth. *1 John 3:18*

⮞ 29 ⮜

WHEN YOUR EMPLOYEES LACK YOUR PASSION

He becometh poor that dealeth with a slack hand: but the hand of the diligent maketh rich. *Proverbs 10:4*

The thoughts of the diligent tend only to plenteousness; but of every one that is hasty only to want. *Proverbs 21:5*

Seest thou a man diligent in his business? he shall stand before kings; he shall not stand before mean men.
Proverbs 22:29

Be thou diligent to know the state of thy flocks, and look well to thy herds.
Proverbs 27:23

Whatsoever thy hand findeth to do, do it with thy might; for there is no work, nor device, nor knowledge, nor wisdom, in the grave, whither thou goest.   *Ecclesiastes 9:10*

Let your light so shine before men, that they may see your good works, and glorify your Father which is in heaven.
Matthew 5:16

But seek ye first the kingdom of God, and His righteousness; and all these things shall be added unto you.   *Matthew 6:33*

I press toward the mark for the prize of the high calling of God in Christ Jesus.
Philippians 3:14

Study to shew thyself approved unto God, a workman that needeth not to be ashamed, rightly dividing the word of truth.
2 Timothy 2:15

For God is not unrighteous to forget your work and labour of love, which ye have shewed toward His name, in that ye have ministered to the saints, and do minister.
Hebrews 6:10

Therefore to him that knoweth to do good, and doeth it not, to him it is sin.
James 4:17

The Questions You Ask Determine The Solutions You Discover.

-MIKE MURDOCK

Copyright © 2001 by Mike Murdock • Wisdom International
The Wisdom Center • P.O. Box 99 • Denton, TX 76202

~ 30 ~

WHEN YOU WANT TO MOTIVATE YOUR STAFF

And the Lord appeared unto him the same night, and said, I am the God of Abraham thy father: fear not, for I am with thee, and will bless thee, and multiply thy seed for My servant Abraham's sake.
Genesis 26:24

Be strong and of a good courage, fear not, nor be afraid of them: for the Lord thy God, He it is that doth go with thee; He will not fail thee, nor forsake thee.
Deuteronomy 31:6

Moreover as for me, God forbid that I should sin against the Lord in ceasing to pray for you: but I will teach you the good and the right way: *1 Samuel 12:23*

And he answered, Fear not: for they that be with us are more than they that be with them. *2 Kings 6:16*

Arise; for this matter belongeth unto thee: we also will be with thee: be of good courage, and do it. *Ezra 10:4*

Then I told them of the hand of my God which was good upon me; as also the king's words that he had spoken unto me. And they said, Let us rise up and build. So they strengthened their hands for this good work.
Nehemiah 2:18

A wise man will hear, and will increase learning; and a man of understanding shall attain unto wise counsels: *Proverbs 1:5*

Give instruction to a wise man, and he will be yet wiser: teach a just man, and he will increase in learning. *Proverbs 9:9*

Two are better than one; because they have a good reward for their labour.
Ecclesiastes 4:9

Fear thou not; for I am with thee: be not dismayed; for I am thy God: I will strengthen thee; yea, I will help thee; yea, I will uphold thee with the right hand of my righteousness. *Isaiah 41:10*

For I the Lord thy God will hold thy right hand, saying unto thee, Fear not; I will help thee. *Isaiah 41:13*

When thou passest through the waters, I will be with thee; and through the rivers, they shall not overflow thee: when thou walkest through the fire, thou shalt not be burned; neither shall the flame kindle upon thee. *Isaiah 43:2*

Fear ye not therefore, ye are of more value than many sparrows. *Matthew 10:31*

But straightway Jesus spake unto them, saying, Be of good cheer; it is I; be not afraid. *Matthew 14:27*

In all things shewing thyself a pattern of good works: in doctrine shewing uncorruptness, gravity, sincerity, *Titus 2:7*

Sound speech, that cannot be condemned; that he that is of the contrary part may be ashamed, having no evil thing to say of you. *Titus 2:8*

~ 31 ~

WHEN YOUR EMPLOYEE FACES TERMINATION

The Lord lift up His countenance upon thee, and give thee peace.   *Numbers 6:26*

For the Lord thy God is a merciful God; He will not forsake thee, neither destroy thee, nor forget the covenant of thy fathers which He sware unto them.
Deuteronomy 4:31

Be strong and of a good courage, fear not, nor be afraid of them: for the Lord thy God, He it is that doth go with thee; He will not fail thee, nor forsake thee.
Deuteronomy 31:6

And the Lord, He it is that doth go before thee; He will be with thee, He will not fail thee, neither forsake thee: fear not, neither be dismayed.   *Deuteronomy 31:8*

I had fainted, unless I had believed to see the goodness of the Lord in the land of the living. *Psalm 27:13*

Wait on the Lord: be of good courage, and he shall strengthen thine heart: wait, I say, on the Lord. *Psalm 27:14*

Make Thy face to shine upon Thy servant: save me for Thy mercies' sake. *Psalm 31:16*

I have been young, and now am old; yet have I not seen the righteous forsaken, nor his seed begging bread. *Psalm 37:25*

Therefore I say unto you, Take no thought for your life, what ye shall eat, or what ye shall drink; nor yet for your body, what ye shall put on. Is not the life more than meat, and the body than raiment? *Matthew 6:25*

Take therefore no thought for the morrow: for the morrow shall take thought for the things of itself. Sufficient unto the day is the evil thereof. *Matthew 6:34*

Now the God of hope fill you with all joy and peace in believing, that ye may abound in hope, through the power of the Holy Ghost. *Romans 15:13*

There hath no temptation taken you but such as is common to man: but God is faithful, who will not suffer you to be tempted above that ye are able; but will with the temptation also make a way to escape, that ye may be able to bear it.
1 Corinthians 10:13

Finally, my brethren, be strong in the Lord, and in the power of His might.
Ephesians 6:10

Not that I speak in respect of want: for I have learned, in whatsoever state I am, therewith to be content. *Philippians 4:11*

I know both how to be abased, and I know how to abound: every where and in all things I am instructed both to be full and to be hungry, both to abound and to suffer need. *Philippians 4:12*

I can do all things through Christ which

strengtheneth me. *Philippians 4:13*

But my God shall supply all your need according to His riches in glory by Christ Jesus. *Philippians 4:19*

Let your conversation be without covetousness; and be content with such things as ye have: for He hath said, I will never leave thee, nor forsake thee.
Hebrews 13:5

That the trial of your faith, being much more precious than of gold that perisheth, though it be tried with fire, might be found unto praise and honour and glory at the appearing of Jesus Christ. *1 Peter 1:7*

Casting all your care upon Him; for He careth for you. *1 Peter 5:7*

32

WHEN YOU LOSE A KEY EMPLOYEE

It shall not seem hard unto thee, when thou sendest him away free from thee; for he hath been worth a double hired servant to thee, in serving thee six years: and the Lord thy God shall bless thee in all that thou doest. *Deuteronomy 15:18*

The eternal God is thy refuge, and underneath are the everlasting arms: and He shall thrust out the enemy from before thee; and shall say, Destroy them.
Deuteronomy 33:27

When Thou saidst, Seek ye My face; my heart said unto Thee, Thy face, Lord, will I seek. *Psalm 27:8*

The steps of a good man are ordered by the Lord: and He delighteth in his way.
Psalm 37:23

Be still, and know that I am God: I will be exalted among the heathen, I will be exalted in the earth. *Psalm 46:10*

And call upon Me in the day of trouble: I will deliver thee, and thou shalt glorify Me. *Psalm 50:15*

Cast thy burden upon the Lord, and He shall sustain thee: He shall never suffer the righteous to be moved. *Psalm 55:22*

My flesh and my heart faileth: but God is the strength of my heart, and my portion for ever. *Psalm 73:26*

In the multitude of my thoughts within me Thy comforts delight my soul. *Psalm 94:19*

He healeth the broken in heart, and bindeth up their wounds. *Psalm 147:3*

Fear thou not; for I am with thee: be not dismayed; for I am thy God: I will strengthen thee; yea, I will help thee; yea, I will uphold thee with the right hand of My righteousness. *Isaiah 41:10*

Behold, all they that were incensed against thee shall be ashamed and

confounded: they shall be as nothing; and they that strive with thee shall perish.
Isaiah 41:11

Thou shalt seek them, and shalt not find them, even them that contended with thee: they that war against thee shall be as nothing, and as a thing of nought.
Isaiah 41:12

For I the Lord thy God will hold thy right hand, saying unto thee, Fear not; I will help thee. *Isaiah 41:13*

In your patience possess ye your souls.
Luke 21:19

Not that I speak in respect of want: for I have learned, in whatsoever state I am, therewith to be content. *Philippians 4:11*

I know both how to be abased, and I know how to abound: every where and in all things I am instructed both to be full and to be hungry, both to abound and to suffer need. *Philippians 4:12*

I can do all things through Christ which strengtheneth me. *Philippians 4:13*

Thou therefore endure hardness, as a good soldier of Jesus Christ. *2 Timothy 2:3*

~ 33 ~

WHEN A COLLEAGUE NEEDS YOUR SUPPORT

A friend loveth at all times, and a brother is born for adversity.   *Proverbs 17:17*

Ointment and perfume rejoice the heart: so doth the sweetness of a man's friend by hearty counsel.   *Proverbs 27:9*

Iron sharpeneth iron; so a man sharpeneth the countenance of his friend.
Proverbs 27:17

As in water face answereth to face, so the heart of man to man.   *Proverbs 27:19*

Two are better than one; because they have a good reward for their labour.
Ecclesiastes 4:9

For if they fall, the one will lift up his fellow: but woe to him that is alone when he falleth; for he hath not another to help him up. *Ecclesiastes 4:10*

But they that wait upon the Lord shall renew their strength; they shall mount up with wings as eagles; they shall run, and not be weary; and they shall walk, and not faint.
Isaiah 40:31

Therefore all things whatsoever ye would that men should do to you, do ye even so to them: for this is the law and the prophets. *Matthew 7:12*

A new commandment I give unto you, That ye love one another; as I have loved you, that ye also love one another.
John 13:34

I have shewed you all things, how that so labouring ye ought to support the weak, and to remember the words of the Lord Jesus, how He said, It is more blessed to give than to receive. *Acts 20:35*

That is, that I may be comforted together with you by the mutual faith both of you and me. *Romans 1:12*

That I may come unto you with joy by the will of God, and may with you be refreshed. *Romans 15:32*

Therefore we were comforted in your comfort: yea, and exceedingly the more joyed we for the joy of Titus, because his spirit was refreshed by you all. *2 Corinthians 7:13*

Bear ye one another's burdens, and so fulfil the law of Christ. *Galatians 6:2*

As we have therefore opportunity, let us do good unto all men, especially unto them who are of the household of faith.
Galatians 6:10

Finally, be ye all of one mind, having compassion one of another, love as brethren, be pitiful, be courteous: *1 Peter 3:8*

Beloved, if God so loved us, we ought also to love one another. *1 John 4:11*

34

WHEN YOUR INSTRUCTIONS ARE IGNORED

The God of Israel said, the Rock of Israel spake to me, He that ruleth over men must be just, ruling in the fear of God.
2 Samuel 23:3

I will not be afraid of ten thousands of people, that have set themselves against me round about. *Psalm 3:6*

But as for me, I will walk in mine integrity: redeem me, and be merciful unto me. *Psalm 26:11*

Though an host should encamp against me, my heart shall not fear: though war should rise against me, in this will I be confident. *Psalm 27:3*

For in the time of trouble He shall hide me in His pavilion: in the secret of His tabernacle shall He hide me; He shall set me up upon a rock. *Psalm 27:5*

God is our refuge and strength, a very present help in trouble.

Therefore will not we fear, though the earth be removed, and though the mountains be carried into the midst of the sea;
Psalm 46:1,2

My flesh and my heart faileth: but God is the strength of my heart, and my portion for ever. *Psalm 73:26*

See then that ye walk circumspectly, not as fools, but as wise, *Ephesians 5:15*

YOUR EMPLOYER

~ 35 ~

WHEN YOUR EMPLOYER SEEMS UNCOMPASSIONATE

I said, I will take heed to my ways, that I sin not with my tongue: I will keep my mouth with a bridle, while the wicked is before me. *Psalm 39:1*

The lip of truth shall be established for ever: but a lying tongue is but for a moment. *Proverbs 12:19*

Whoso keepeth his mouth and his tongue keepeth his soul from troubles. *Proverbs 21:23*

Answer not a fool according to his folly, lest thou also be like unto him. *Proverbs 26:4*

But I say unto you, That ye resist not evil: but whosoever shall smite thee on thy

right cheek, turn to him the other also.
Matthew 5:39

Give to him that asketh thee, and from him that would borrow of thee turn not thou away. *Matthew 5:42*

O generation of vipers, how can ye, being evil, speak good things? for out of the abundance of the heart the mouth speaketh.
A good man out of the good treasure of the heart bringeth forth good things: and an evil man out of the evil treasure bringeth forth evil things. *Matthew 12:34,35*

Recompense to no man evil for evil. Provide things honest in the sight of all men.
Romans 12:17

If it be possible, as much as lieth in you, live peaceably with all men. *Romans 12:18*

Dearly beloved, avenge not yourselves, but rather give place unto wrath: for it is written, Vengeance is Mine; I will repay, saith the Lord. *Romans 12:19*

Be not overcome of evil, but overcome evil with good. *Romans 12:21*

See that none render evil for evil unto any man; but ever follow that which is good, both among yourselves, and to all men.
1 Thessalonians 5:15

Follow peace with all men, and holiness, without which no man shall see the Lord:
Hebrews 12:14

But the wisdom that is from above is first pure, then peaceable, gentle, and easy to be intreated, full of mercy and good fruits, without partiality, and without hypocrisy.
James 3:17

And the fruit of righteousness is sown in peace of them that make peace.
James 3:18

For this is thankworthy, if a man for conscience toward God endure grief, suffering wrongfully. *1 Peter 2:19*

For what glory is it, if, when ye be buffeted for your faults, ye shall take it patiently? but if, when ye do well, and suffer for it, ye take it patiently, this is acceptable with God. *1 Peter 2:20*

Losers Focus On What They Are Going Through While Champions Focus On What They Are Going To.

—MIKE MURDOCK

Copyright © 2001 by Mike Murdock • Wisdom International
The Wisdom Center • P.O. Box 99 • Denton, TX 76202

36

WHEN YOUR EMPLOYER CREATES YOUR STRESS

One man of you shall chase a thousand: for the Lord your God, He it is that fighteth for you, as He hath promised you.

Joshua 23:10

He will keep the feet of His saints, and the wicked shall be silent in darkness; for by strength shall no man prevail.

1 Samuel 2:9

And he said, Hearken ye, all Judah, and ye inhabitants of Jerusalem, and thou king Jehoshaphat, Thus saith the Lord unto you, Be not afraid nor dismayed by reason of this great multitude; for the battle is not yours, but God's.

2 Chronicles 20:15

But Thou, O Lord, art a shield for me; my glory, and the lifter up of mine head.

Psalm 3:3

My voice shalt Thou hear in the morning, O Lord; in the morning will I direct my prayer unto Thee, and will look up.
Psalm 5:3

For the Lord shall be thy confidence, and shall keep thy foot from being taken.
Proverbs 3:26

Let thine eyes look right on, and let thine eyelids look straight before thee.
Proverbs 4:25

In the fear of the Lord is strong confidence: and His children shall have a place of refuge. *Proverbs 14:26*

He giveth power to the faint; and to them that have no might He increaseth strength. *Isaiah 40:29*

But they that wait upon the Lord shall renew their strength; they shall mount up with wings as eagles; they shall run, and not be weary; and they shall walk, and not faint.
Isaiah 40:31

Fear thou not; for I am with thee: be

not dismayed; for I am thy God: I will strengthen thee; yea, I will help thee; yea, I will uphold thee with the right hand of My righteousness. *Isaiah 41:10*

When thou passest through the waters, I will be with thee; and through the rivers, they shall not overflow thee: when thou walkest through the fire, thou shalt not be burned; neither shall the flame kindle upon thee. *Isaiah 43:2*

Then he answered and spake unto me, saying, This is the word of the Lord unto Zerubbabel, saying, Not by might, nor by power, but by My spirit, saith the Lord of hosts. *Zechariah 4:6*

The Lord knoweth how to deliver the godly out of temptations, and to reserve the unjust unto the day of judgment to be punished: *2 Peter 2:9*

37

WHEN YOUR EMPLOYER DISAPPOINTS YOU

Thou shalt not avenge, nor bear any grudge against the children of thy people, but thou shalt love thy neighbour as thyself: I am the Lord. *Leviticus 19:18*

O Lord my God, in Thee do I put my trust: save me from all them that persecute me, and deliver me: *Psalm 7:1*

Lest he tear my soul like a lion, rending it in pieces, while there is none to deliver. *Psalm 7:2*

O my God, I trust in Thee: let me not be ashamed, let not mine enemies triumph over me. *Psalm 25:2*

Trust in the Lord, and do good; so shalt thou dwell in the land, and verily thou shalt be fed. *Psalm 37:3*

Delight thyself also in the Lord; and He shall give thee the desires of thine heart.
Psalm 37:4

Commit thy way unto the Lord; trust also in Him; and He shall bring it to pass.
Psalm 37:5

And He shall bring forth thy righteousness as the light, and thy judgment as the noonday. *Psalm 37:6*

Cease from anger, and forsake wrath: fret not thyself in any wise to do evil.
Psalm 37:8

Say not thou, I will recompense evil; but wait on the Lord, and He shall save thee.
Proverbs 20:22

For My name's sake will I defer Mine anger, and for My praise will I refrain for thee, that I cut thee not off. *Isaiah 48:9*

For if ye forgive men their trespasses, your heavenly Father will also forgive you:
Matthew 6:14

And if he trespass against thee seven times in a day, and seven times in a day turn again to thee, saying, I repent; thou shalt forgive him. *Luke 17:4*

Recompense to no man evil for evil. Provide things honest in the sight of all men.
Romans 12:17

But we were gentle among you, even as a nurse cherisheth her children:
1 Thessalonians 2:7

And the servant of the Lord must not strive; but be gentle unto all men, apt to teach, patient, *2 Timothy 2:24*

And the Lord shall deliver me from every evil work, and will preserve me unto His heavenly kingdom: to whom be glory for ever and ever. Amen. *2 Timothy 4:18*

To speak evil of no man, to be no brawlers, but gentle, shewing all meekness unto all men. *Titus 3:2*

All Men Fall...
The Great Ones Get Back Up.

-MIKE MURDOCK

Copyright © 2001 by Mike Murdock • Wisdom International
The Wisdom Center • P.O. Box 99 • Denton, TX 76202

38

WHEN YOU HAVE MADE A COSTLY MISTAKE

For the Lord thy God is a merciful God; He will not forsake thee, neither destroy thee, nor forget the covenant of thy fathers which He sware unto them.
Deuteronomy 4:31

And thou shalt return and obey the voice of the Lord, and do all His commandments which I command thee this day.
Deuteronomy 30:8

And David's heart smote him after that he had numbered the people. And David said unto the Lord, I have sinned greatly in that I have done: and now, I beseech thee, O Lord, take away the iniquity of thy servant; for I have done very foolishly.   *2 Samuel 24:10*

If My people, which are called by My name, shall humble themselves, and pray,

and seek My face, and turn from their wicked ways; then will I hear from heaven, and will forgive their sin, and will heal their land.
2 Chronicles 7:14

If iniquity be in thine hand, put it far away, and let not wickedness dwell in thy tabernacles. *Job 11:14*

If thou return to the Almighty, thou shalt be built up, thou shalt put away iniquity far from thy tabernacles. *Job 22:23*

That which I see not teach Thou me: if I have done iniquity, I will do no more.
Job 34:32

Create in me a clean heart, O God; and renew a right spirit within me. *Psalm 51:10*

The sacrifices of God are a broken spirit: a broken and a contrite heart, O God, Thou wilt not despise. *Psalm 51:17*

Turn you at My reproof: behold, I will pour out My spirit unto you, I will make known My words unto you. *Proverbs 1:23*

He that covereth his sins shall not prosper: but whoso confesseth and forsaketh them shall have mercy. *Proverbs 28:13*

For thus saith the high and lofty One that inhabiteth eternity, whose name is Holy; I dwell in the high and holy place, with him also that is of a contrite and humble spirit, to revive the spirit of the humble, and to revive the heart of the contrite ones.
Isaiah 57:15

And I will restore to you the years that the locust hath eaten, the cankerworm, and the caterpillar, and the palmerworm, my great army which I sent among you.
Joel 2:25

And ye shall eat in plenty, and be satisfied, and praise the name of the Lord your God, that hath dealt wondrously with you: and My people shall never be ashamed.
Joel 2:26

If we confess our sins, He is faithful and just to forgive us our sins, and to cleanse us from all unrighteousness. *1 John 1:9*

The Pursuit
   Of The Mentor
Reveals The Passion
   Of The Protégé.

-MIKE MURDOCK

Copyright © 2001 by Mike Murdock • Wisdom International
The Wisdom Center • P.O. Box 99 • Denton, TX 76202

39

WHEN YOU FEEL UNQUALIFIED

And Caleb stilled the people before Moses, and said, Let us go up at once, and possess it; for we are well able to overcome it. *Numbers 13:30*

Be ye strong therefore, and let not your hands be weak: for your work shall be rewarded. *2 Chronicles 15:7*

Be of good courage, and He shall strengthen your heart, all ye that hope in the Lord. *Psalm 31:24*

Counsel is mine, and sound wisdom: I am understanding; I have strength.
Proverbs 8:14

And by knowledge shall the chambers be filled with all precious and pleasant riches. *Proverbs 24*

A wise man is strong; yea, a man of knowledge increaseth strength.
Proverbs 24:5

Wisdom strengtheneth the wise more than ten mighty men which are in the city.
Ecclesiastes 7:19

If the iron be blunt, and he do not whet the edge, then must he put to more strength: but wisdom is profitable to direct.
Ecclesiastes 10:10

Strengthen ye the weak hands, and confirm the feeble knees. *Isaiah 35:3*

Say to them that are of a fearful heart, Be strong, fear not: behold, your God will come with vengeance, even God with a recompence; He will come and save you.
Isaiah 35:4

Fear thou not; for I am with thee: be not dismayed; for I am thy God: I will strengthen thee; yea, I will help thee; yea, I will uphold thee with the right hand of My righteousness. *Isaiah 41:10*

He staggered not at the promise of God through unbelief; but was strong in faith, giving glory to God; *Romans 4:20*

And being fully persuaded that, what He had promised, He was able also to perform. *Romans 4:21*

But God hath chosen the foolish things of the world to confound the wise; and God hath chosen the weak things of the world to confound the things which are mighty;
1 Corinthians 1:27

For to one is given by the Spirit the word of Wisdom; to another the word of knowledge by the same Spirit; *1 Corinthians 12:8*

And God is able to make all grace abound toward you; that ye, always having all sufficiency in all things, may abound to every good work: *2 Corinthians 9:8*

And He said unto me, My grace is sufficient for thee: for My strength is made perfect in weakness. Most gladly therefore will I rather glory in my infirmities, that the power of Christ may rest upon me.
2 Corinthians 12:9

Therefore I take pleasure in infirmities, in reproaches, in necessities, in persecutions, in distresses for Christ's sake: for when I am weak, then am I strong.
2 Corinthians 12:10

That He would grant you, according to the riches of His glory, to be strengthened with might by His Spirit in the inner man;
Ephesians 3:16

Now unto Him that is able to do exceeding abundantly above all that we ask or think, according to the power that worketh in us, *Ephesians 3:20*

I can do all things through Christ which strengtheneth me. *Philippians 4:13*

If any of you lack wisdom, let him ask of God, that giveth to all men liberally, and upbraideth not; and it shall be given him.
James 1:5

Your Family

~ 40 ~

When You Face Marital Problems

And Adam said, This is now bone of my bones, and flesh of my flesh: she shall be called Woman, because she was taken out of Man. *Genesis 2:23*

Therefore shall a man leave his father and his mother, and shall cleave unto his wife: and they shall be one flesh.
Genesis 2:24

I laid me down and slept; I awaked; for the Lord sustained me. *Psalm 3:5*

Have mercy upon me, O Lord; for I am weak: O Lord, heal me; for my bones are vexed. *Psalm 6:2*

The discretion of a man deferreth his anger; and it is his glory to pass over a transgression. *Proverbs 19:11*

So shall they fear the name of the Lord from the west, and His glory from the rising of the sun. When the enemy shall come in like a flood, the Spirit of the Lord shall lift up a standard against him. *Isaiah 59:19*

Blessed are the merciful: for they shall obtain mercy. *Matthew 5:7*

It hath been said, Whosoever shall put away his wife, let him give her a writing of divorcement: *Matthew 5:31*

But I say unto you, That whosoever shall put away his wife, saving for the cause of fornication, causeth her to commit adultery: and whosoever shall marry her that is divorced committeth adultery.
Matthew 5:32

What therefore God hath joined together, let not man put asunder.
Mark 10:9

Be ye therefore merciful, as your Father also is merciful. *Luke 6:36*

Judge not, and ye shall not be judged: condemn not, and ye shall not be condemned: forigve, and ye shall be forgiven: *Luke 6:37*

And forgive us our sins; for we also forgive every one that is indebted to us. And lead us not into temptation; but deliver us from evil. *Luke 11:4*

Be not overcome of evil, but overcome evil with good. *Romans 12:21*

So ought men to love their wives as their own bodies. He that loveth his wife loveth himself. *Ephesians 5:28*

For no man ever yet hated his own flesh; but nourisheth and cherisheth it, even as the Lord the church: *Ephesians 5:29*

Nevertheless let every one of you in particular so love his wife even as himself; and the wife see that she reverence her husband. *Ephesians 5:33*

Marriage is honourable in all, and the bed undefiled: but whoremongers and adulterers God will judge.   *Hebrews 13:4*

If any of you lack wisdom, let him ask of God, that giveth to all men liberally, and upbraideth not; and it shall be given him.
James 1:5

Confess your faults one to another, and pray one for another, that ye may be healed. The effectual fervent prayer of a righteous man availeth much.   *James 5:16*

~ 41 ~

WHEN YOUR SPOUSE IS UNSUPPORTIVE

The Lord is my light and my salvation; whom shall I fear? the Lord is my strength of my life; of whom shall I be afraid?
Psalm 27:1

Though an host should encamp against me, my heart shall not fear; though war should rise against me, in this will I be confident. *Psalm 27:3*

Wait on the Lord: be of good courage, and He shall strengthen thine heart; wait, I say, on the Lord. *Psalm 27:14*

For Thou art my rock and my fortress; therefore for Thy name's sake lead me, and guide me. *Psalm 31:3*

Pull me out of the net that they have laid privily for me: for Thou art my strength.
Psalm 31:4

Thou art my hiding place; Thou shalt preserve me from trouble; Thou shalt compass me about with songs of deliverance.
Psalm 32:7

I will instruct thee and teach thee in the way which thou shalt go: I will guide thee with Mine eye. *Psalm 32:8*

My soul melteth for heaviness: strengthen thou me according unto Thy word. *Psalm 119:28*

Hatred stirreth up strifes: but love covereth all sins. *Proverbs 10:12*

Finally, brethren, whatsoever things are true, whatsoever things are honest, whatsoever things are just, whatsoever things are pure, whatsoever things are lovely, whatsoever things are of good report; if there be any virtue, and if there be any praise, think on these things. *Philippians 4:8*

I know both how to be abased, and I know how to abound: every where and in all things I am instructed both to be full and to be hungry, both to abound and to suffer need. *Philippians 4:12*

I can do all things through Christ which strengtheneth me. *Philippians 4:13*

But my God shall supply all your need according to His riches in glory by Christ Jesus. *Philippians 4:19*

Put on therefore, as the elect of God, holy and beloved, bowels of mercies, kindness, humbleness of mind, meekness, longsuffering; *Colossians 3:12*

Forbearing one another, and forgiving one another, if any man have a quarrel against any: even as Christ forgave you, so also do ye. *Colossians 3:13*

And above all these things put on charity, which is the bond of perfectness.
Colossians 3:14

If any of you lack wisdom, let him ask of God, that giveth to all men liberally, and upbraideth not; and it shall be given him.
James 1:5

But if ye have bitter envying and strife in your hearts, glory not, and lie not against the truth. *James 3:14*

For where envying and strife is, there is confusion and every evil work.
James 3:16

But the wisdom that is from above is first pure, then peaceable, gentle, and easy to be intreated, full of mercy and good fruits, without partiality, and without hypocrisy.
James 3:17

And the fruit of righteousness is sown in peace of them that make peace.
James 3:18

Confess your faults one to another, and pray one for another, that ye may be healed. The effectual fervent prayer of a righteous man availeth much. *James 5:16*

42

WHEN A FAMILY MEMBER FACES SICKNESS

And said, If thou wilt diligently hearken to the voice of the Lord thy God, and wilt do that which is right in His sight, and wilt give ear to His commandments, and keep all His statutes, I will put none of these diseases upon thee, which I have brought upon the Egyptians: for I am the Lord that healeth thee. *Exodus 15:26*

And the Lord will take away from thee all sickness, and will put none of the evil diseases of Egypt, which thou knowest, upon thee; but will lay them upon all them that hate thee. *Deuteronomy 7:15*

Have mercy upon me, O Lord; for I am weak: O Lord, heal me; for my bones are vexed. *Psalm 6:2*

Forsake me not, O Lord: O my God, be not far from me. *Psalm 38:21*

Bless the Lord, O my soul, and forget not all His benefits: *Psalm 103:2*

Who forgiveth all thine iniquities; who healeth all thy diseases; *Psalm 103:3*

Let thy tender mercies come unto me, that I may live: for Thy law is my delight.
Psalm 119:77

For they are life unto those that find them, and health to all their flesh.
Proverbs 4:22

Surely He hath borne our griefs, and carried our sorrows: yet we did esteem Him stricken, smitten of God, and afflicted.
Isaiah 53:4

But He was wounded for our transgressions, He was bruised for our iniquities: the chastisement of our peace was upon Him; and with His stripes we are healed. *Isaiah 53:5*

For I will restore health unto thee, and I will heal thee of thy wounds, saith the Lord; because they called thee an Outcast, saying, This is Zion, whom no man seeketh after.
Jeremiah 30:17

And Jesus saith unto him, I will come and heal him. *Matthew 8:7*

Humble yourselves in the sight of the Lord, and He shall lift you up. *James 4:10*

Is any among you afflicted? let him pray. Is any merry? let him sing psalms. *James 5:13*

Is any sick among you? let him call for the elders of the church; and let them pray over him, anointing him with oil in the name of the Lord: *James 5:14*

And the prayer of faith shall save the sick, and the Lord shall raise him up; and if he have committed sins, they shall be forgiven him. *James 5:15*

Confess your faults one to another, and pray one for another, that ye may be healed. The effectual fervent prayer of a righteous man availeth much. *James 5:16*

43

WHEN YOUR FAMILY TIME IS INADEQUATE

Only take heed to thyself, and keep thy soul diligently, lest thou forget the things which thine eyes have seen, and lest they depart from thy heart all the days of thy life: but teach them thy sons, and thy sons' sons;
Deuteronomy 4:9

And these words, which I command thee this day, shall be in thine heart:
Deuteronomy 6:6

And thou shalt teach them diligently unto thy children, and shalt talk of them when thou sittest in thine house, and when thou walkest by the way, and when thou liest down, and when thou risest up.
Deuteronomy 6:7

And ye shall teach them your children, speaking of them when thou sittest in thine house, and when thou walkest by the way, when thou liest down, and when thou risest up. *Deuteronomy 11:19*

For He established a testimony in Jacob, and appointed a law in Israel, which He commanded our fathers, that they should make them known to their children:
Psalm 78:5

That the generation to come might know them, even the children which should be born; who should arise and declare them to their children: *Psalm 78:6*

That they might set their hope in God, and not forget the works of God, but keep His commandments: *Psalm 78:7*

A good man leaveth an inheritance to his children's children: and the wealth of the sinner is laid up for the just.
Proverbs 13:22

The just man walketh in his integrity: his children are blessed after him.
Proverbs 20:7

Train up a child in the way he should go: and when he is old, he will not depart from it. *Proverbs 22:6*

Through wisdom is an house builded; and by understanding it is established:
Proverbs 24:3

Correct thy son, and he shall give thee rest; yea, he shall give delight unto thy soul.
Proverbs 29:17

Tell ye your children of it, and let your children tell their children, and their children another generation. *Joel 1:3*

But seek ye first the kingdom of God, and his righteousness; and all these things shall be added unto you. *Matthew 6:33*

And, ye fathers, provoke not your children to wrath: but bring them up in the nurture and admonition of the Lord.
Ephesians 6:4

Fathers, provoke not your children to anger, lest they be discouraged.
Colossians 3:21

But if any provide not for his own, and specially for those of his own house, he hath denied the faith, and is worse than an infidel.
1 Timothy 5:8

44

WHEN YOUR WORK SCHEDULE INTERFERES WITH YOUR SPIRITUAL LIFE

And he went out to meet Asa, and said unto him, Hear ye me, Asa, and all Judah and Benjamin; The Lord is with you, while ye be with Him; and if ye seek Him, He will be found of you; but if ye forsake Him, He will forsake you. *2 Chronicles 15:2*

For I was envious at the foolish, when I saw the prosperity of the wicked.
Psalm 73:3

When I thought to know this, it was too painful for me; *Psalm 73:16*

Until I went into the sanctuary of God; then understood I their end. *Psalm 73:17*

But it is good for me to draw near to God: I have put my trust in the Lord God,

that I may declare all Thy works.
Psalm 73:28

The Lord is nigh unto all them that call upon Him, to all that call upon Him in truth.
Psalm 145:18

Seek ye the Lord while He may be found, call ye upon Him while He is near:
Isaiah 55:6

They shall enter into My sanctuary, and they shall come near to My table, to minister unto Me, and they shall keep My charge.
Ezekiel 44:16

But seek ye first the kingdom of God, and His righteousness; and all these things shall be added unto you.   *Matthew 6:33*

This people draweth nigh unto Me with their mouth, and honoureth Me with their lips; but their heart is far from Me.
Matthew 15:8

And the cares of this world, and the deceitfulness of riches, and the lusts of other things entering in, choke the word, and it becometh unfruitful. *Mark 4:19*

And that which fell among thorns are they, which, when they have heard, go forth, and are choked with cares and riches and pleasures of this life, and bring no fruit to perfection. *Luke 8:14*

And take heed to yourselves, lest at any time your hearts be overcharged with surfeiting, and drunkenness, and cares of this life, and so that day come upon you unawares. *Luke 21:34*

Ye did run well; who did hinder you that ye should not obey the truth? *Galatians 5:7*

Neglect not the gift that is in thee, which was given thee by prophecy, with the laying on of the hands of the presbytery.
1 Timothy 4:14

How shall we escape, if we neglect so great salvation; which at the first began to be spoken by the Lord, and was confirmed unto us by them that heard Him;
Hebrews 2:3

Let us hold fast the profession of our faith without wavering; for He is faithful that promised; *Hebrews 10:23*

Not forsaking the assembling of ourselves together, as the manner of some is; but exhorting one another: and so much the more, as ye see the day approaching.
Hebrews 10:25

Looking unto Jesus the author and finisher of our faith; Who for the joy that was set before Him endured the cross, despising the shame, and is set down at the right hand of the throne of God. *Hebrews 12:2*

Draw nigh to God, and He will draw nigh to you. Cleanse your hands, ye sinners; and purify your hearts, ye double minded.
James 4:8

Your Finances

≈ 45 ≈

When It Seems Impossible To Pay Your Bills

The steps of a good man are ordered by the Lord: and he delighteth in His way.
Psalm 37:23

Though he fall, he shall not be utterly cast down: for the Lord upholdeth him with His hand. *Psalm 37:24*

He will regard the prayer of the destitute, and not despise their prayer.
Psalm 102:17

So shall thy barns be filled with plenty, and thy presses shall burst out with new wine. *Proverbs 3:10*

Remove far from me vanity and lies: give me neither poverty nor riches; feed me with food convenient for me: *Proverbs 30:8*

Lest I be full, and deny Thee, and say, Who is the Lord? or lest I be poor, and steal, and take the name of my God in vain.
Proverbs 30:9

Although the fig tree shall not blossom, neither shall fruit be in the vines; the labour of the olive shall fail, and the fields shall yield no meat; the flock shall be cut off from the fold, and there shall be no herd in the stalls: *Habakkuk 3:17*

Yet I will rejoice in the Lord, I will joy in the God of my salvation. *Habakkuk 3:18*

Ye are cursed with a curse: for ye have robbed Me, even this whole nation.
Bring ye all the tithes into the storehouse, that there may be meat in Mine house, and prove Me now herewith, saith the Lord of hosts, if I will not open you the windows of heaven, and pour you out a blessing, that there shall not be room enough to receive it. *Malachi 3:9,10*

Therefore I say unto you, Take no thought for your life, what ye shall eat, or what ye shall drink; nor yet for your body,

what ye shall put on. Is not the life more than meat, and the body than raiment?
Matthew 6:25

Wherefore, if God so clothe the grass of the field, which today is, and tomorrow is cast into the oven, shall He not much more clothe you, O ye of little faith? *Matthew 6:30*

But seek ye first the kingdom of God, and His righteousness; and all these things shall be added unto you. *Matthew 6:33*

Give, and it shall be given unto you; good measure, pressed down, and shaken together, and running over, shall men give into your bosom. For with the same measure that ye mete withal it shall be measured to you again. *Luke 6:38*

And we know that all things work together for good to them that love God, to them who are the called according to His purpose. *Romans 8:28*

But this I say, He which soweth sparingly shall reap also sparingly; and he which soweth bountifully shall reap also bountifully. *2 Corinthians 9:6*

Be careful for nothing; but in every thing by prayer and supplication with thanksgiving let your requests be made known unto God. *Philippians 4:6*

Not that I speak in respect of want: for I have learned, in whatsoever state I am, therewith to be content. *Philippians 4:11*

I know both how to be abased, and I know how to abound: every where and in all things I am instructed both to be full and to be hungry, both to abound and to suffer need. *Philippians 4:12*

Casting all your care upon Him; for He careth for you. *1 Peter 5:7*

46

When You Need A Financial Plan

For Thou art my lamp, O Lord: and the Lord will lighten my darkness.
2 Samuel 22:29

Blessed is the man that walketh not in the counsel of the ungodly, nor standeth in the way of sinners, nor sitteth in the seat of the scornful. *Psalm 1:1*

Lead me in Thy truth, and teach me: for Thou art the God of my salvation; on Thee do I wait all the day. *Psalm 25:5*

The meek will He guide in judgment: and the meek will He teach His way.
Psalm 25:9

What man is he that feareth the Lord? him shall He teach in the way that He shall choose. *Psalm 25:12*

Teach me Thy way, O Lord, and lead me in a plain path, because of mine enemies.
Psalm 27:11

For Thou art my rock and my fortress; therefore for Thy name's sake lead me, and guide me. *Psalm 31:3*

I will instruct thee and teach thee in the way which thou shalt go: I will guide thee with Mine eye. *Psalm 32:8*

Thou shalt guide me with Thy counsel, and afterward receive me to glory.
Psalm 73:24

Turn you at My reproof: behold, I will pour out My spirit unto you, I will make known My words unto you. *Proverbs 1:23*

For the Lord giveth wisdom: out of His mouth cometh knowledge and understanding. *Proverbs 2:6*

I lead in the way of righteousness, in the midst of the paths of judgment:
Proverbs 8:20

That I may cause those that love Me to inherit substance; and I will fill their treasures. *Proverbs 8:21*

In the morning sow thy seed, and in the evening withhold not thine hand: for thou knowest not whether shall prosper, either this or that, or whether they both shall be alike good. *Ecclesiastes 11:6*

And I will bring the blind by a way that they knew not; I will lead them in paths that they have not known: I will make darkness light before them, and crooked things straight. These things will I do unto them, and not forsake them. *Isaiah 42:16*

And the Lord shall guide thee continually, and satisfy thy soul in drought, and make fat thy bones: and thou shalt be like a watered garden, and like a spring of water, whose waters fail not. *Isaiah 58:11*

Call unto Me, and I will answer thee, and shew thee great and mighty things, which thou knowest not. *Jeremiah 33:3*

Give, and it shall be given unto you;

good measure, pressed down, and shaken together, and running over, shall men give into your bosom. For with the same measure that ye mete withal it shall be measured to you again. *Luke 6:38*

For to one is given by the Spirit the word of wisdom; to another the word of knowledge by the same Spirit; *1 Corinthians 12:8*

Beloved, I wish above all things that thou mayest prosper and be in health, even as thy soul prospereth. *3 John 1:2*

47

WHEN YOU FACE A VOLATILE ECONOMY

And they rose early in the morning, and went forth into the wilderness of Tekoa: and as they went forth, Jehosaphat stood and said, Hear me, O Judah, and ye inhabitants of Jerusalem; Believe in the Lord your God, so shall ye be established; believe His prophets, so shall ye prosper.
2 Chronicles 20:20

Truly my soul waiteth upon God: from Him cometh my salvation. *Psalm 62:1*

He only is my rock and my salvation; He is my defence; I shall not be greatly moved. *Psalm 62:2*

And let the beauty of the Lord our God be upon us: and establish Thou the work of our hands upon us; yea, the work of our hands establish Thou it. *Psalm 90:17*

A good man sheweth favour, and lendeth: he will guide his affairs with discretion. *Psalm 112:5*

Surely he shall not be moved for ever: the righteous shall be in everlasting remembrance. *Psalm 112:6*

He shall not be afraid of evil tidings; his heart is fixed, trusting in the Lord.
Psalm 112:7

His heart is established, he shall not be afraid, until he see his desire upon his enemies. *Psalm 112:8*

I will lift up mine eyes unto the hills, from whence cometh my help. *Psalm 121:1*

My help cometh from the Lord, which made heaven and earth. *Psalm 121:2*

He will not suffer thy foot to be moved: He that keepeth thee will not slumber.
Psalm 121:3

Without counsel purposes are disappointed: but in the multitude of

counsellors they are established.
Proverbs 15:22

Commit thy works unto the Lord, and thy thoughts shall be established.
Proverbs 16:3

Every purpose is established by counsel: and with good advice make war.
Proverbs 20:18

Thou wilt keep him in perfect peace, whose mind is stayed on Thee: because he trusteth in Thee.   *Isaiah 26:3*

Therefore thus saith the Lord God, Behold, I lay in Zion for a foundation a stone, a tried stone, a precious corner stone, a sure foundation: he that believeth shall not make haste.   *Isaiah 28:16*

He is like a man which built an house, and digged deep, and laid the foundation on a rock: and when the flood arose, the stream beat vehemently upon that house, and could not shake it: for it was founded upon a rock.
Luke 6:48

But he that heareth, and doeth not, is

like a man that without a foundation built an house upon the earth; against which the stream did beat vehemently, and immediately it fell; and the ruin of that house was great. *Luke 6:49*

And I say unto you, Ask, and it shall be given you; seek, and ye shall find; knock, and it shall be opened unto you. *Luke 11:9*

For every one that asketh receiveth; and he that seeketh findeth; and to him that knocketh it shall be opened. *Luke 11:10*

And be not conformed to this world: but be ye transformed by the renewing of your mind, that ye may prove what is that good, and acceptable, and perfect, will of God.
Romans 12:2

48

When You Are Tempted Toward Dishonesty

Beware that thou forget not the Lord thy God, in not keeping His commandments, and His judgments, and His statutes, which I command thee this day: *Deuteronomy 8:11*

But thou shalt remember the Lord thy God: for it is He that giveth thee power to get wealth, that He may establish His covenant which He sware unto thy fathers, as it is this day.   *Deuteronomy 8:18*

Unless the Lord had been my help, my soul had almost dwelt in silence.
Psalm 94:17

When I said, My foot slippeth; Thy mercy, O Lord, held me up.   *Psalm 94:18*

My son, if sinners entice thee, consent thou not.   *Proverbs 1:10*

My son, walk not thou in the way with them; refrain thy foot from their path:
Proverbs 1:15

Enter not into the path of the wicked, and go not in the way of evil men.
Proverbs 4:14

He that walketh righteously, and speaketh uprightly; he that despiseth the gain of oppressions, that shaketh his hands from holding of bribes, that stoppeth his ears from hearing of blood, and shutteth his eyes from seeing evil; *Isaiah 33:15*

Wherefore if thy hand or thy foot offend thee, cut them off, and cast them from thee: it is better for thee to enter into life halt or maimed, rather than having two hands or two feet to be cast into everlasting fire.
Matthew 18:8

And if thine eye offend thee, pluck it out, and cast it from thee: it is better for thee to enter into life with one eye, rather than having two eyes to be cast into hell fire.
Matthew 18:9

Watch and pray, that ye enter not into

temptation: the spirit indeed is willing, but the flesh is weak. *Matthew 26:41*

Let not sin therefore reign in your mortal body, that ye should obey it in the lusts thereof. *Romans 6:12*

Neither yield ye your members as instruments of unrighteousness unto sin: but yield yourselves unto God, as those that are alive from the dead, and your members as instruments of righteousness unto God. *Romans 6:13*

There hath no temptation taken you but such as is common to man: but God is faithful, who will not suffer you to be tempted above that ye are able; but will with the temptation also make a way to escape, that ye may be able to bear it. *1 Corinthians 10:13*

Watch ye, stand fast in the faith, quit you like men, be strong. *1 Corinthians 16:13*

Let him that stole steal no more: but rather let him labour, working with his hands the thing which is good, that he may have to give to him that needeth.
Ephesians 4:28

Let no man say when he is tempted, I am tempted of God: for God cannot be tempted with evil, neither tempteth He any man: *James 1:13*

But every man is tempted, when he is drawn away of his own lust, and enticed.
James 1:14

Then when lust hath conceived, it bringeth forth sin: and sin, when it is finished, bringeth forth death. *James 1:15*

Do not err, my beloved brethren.
James 1:16

Submit yourselves therefore to God. Resist the devil, and he will flee from you.
James 4:7

～ 49 ～

WHEN TITHING SEEMS TOO DIFFICULT

The gold for things of gold, and the silver for things of silver, and for all manner of work to be made by the hands of artificers. And who then is willing to consecrate his service this day unto the Lord?
1 Chronicles 29:5

Be ye strong therefore, and let not your hands be weak: for your work shall be rewarded.   *2 Chronicles 15:7*

Vow, and pay unto the Lord your God: let all that be round about Him bring presents unto Him that ought to be feared.
Psalm 76:11

A good man sheweth favour, and lendeth: He will guide his affairs with discretion.   *Psalm 112:5*

He hath dispersed, He hath given to the poor; His righteousness endureth for ever; His horn shall be exalted with honour.
Psalm 112:9

Honour the Lord with thy substance, and with the firstfruits of all thine increase:
Proverbs 3:9

So shall thy barns be filled with plenty, and thy presses shall burst out with new wine. *Proverbs 3:10*

He that hath pity upon the poor lendeth unto the Lord; and that which he hath given will He pay him again. *Proverbs 19:17*

He coveteth greedily all the day long: but the righteous giveth and spareth not.
Proverbs 21:26

He that hath a bountiful eye shall be blessed; for he giveth of his bread to the poor.
Proverbs 22:9

He that giveth unto the poor shall not lack: but he that hideth his eyes shall have many a curse. *Proverbs 28:27*

Cast thy bread upon the waters: for thou shalt find it after many days.
Ecclesiastes 11:1

Bring ye all the tithes into the storehouse, that there may be meat in Mine house, and prove Me now herewith, saith the Lord of hosts, if I will not open you the windows of heaven, and pour you out a blessing, that there shall not be room enough to receive it. *Malachi 3:10*

And I will rebuke the devourer for your sakes, and he shall not destroy the fruits of your ground; neither shall your vine cast her fruit before the time in the field, saith the Lord of hosts. *Malachi 3:11*

Give, and it shall be given unto you; good measure, pressed down, and shaken together, and running over, shall men give into your bosom. For with the same measure that ye mete withal it shall be measured to you again. *Luke 6:38*

Upon the first day of the week let every one of you lay by him in store, as God hath proposed him, that there be no gatherings when I come. *1 Corinthians 16:2*

But this I say, He which soweth sparingly shall reap also sparingly; and he which soweth bountifully shall reap also bountifully. *2 Corinthians 9:6*

Every man according as he purposeth in his heart, so let him give; not grudgingly, or of necessity: for God loveth a cheerful giver. *2 Corinthians 9:7*

And God is able to make all grace abound toward you; that ye, always having all sufficiency in all things, may abound to every good work: *2 Corinthians 9:8*

Charge them that are rich in this world, that they be not highminded, nor trust in uncertain riches, but in the living God, who giveth us richly all things to enjoy;
1 Timothy 6:17

That they do good, that they be rich in good works, ready to distribute, willing to communicate; *1 Timothy 6:18*

Laying up in store for themselves a good foundation against the time to come, that they may lay hold on eternal life.
1 Timothy 6:19

But whoso hath this world's good, and seeth his brother have need, and shutteth up his bowels of compassion from him, how dwelleth the love of God in him?
1 John 3:17

My little children, let us not love in word, neither in tongue; but in deed and in truth. *1 John 3:18*

50

WHEN YOU WANT TO GENERATE VENTURE CAPITAL

And God blessed them, and God said unto them, Be fruitful, and multiply, and replenish the earth, and subdue it: and have dominion over the fish of the sea, and over the fowl of the air, and over every living thing that moveth upon the earth.

And God said, Behold, I have given you every herb bearing seed, which is upon the face of all the earth, and every tree, in the which is the fruit of a tree yielding seed; to you it shall be for meat. *Genesis 1:28,29*

But thou shalt remember the Lord thy God: for it is He that giveth thee power to get wealth, that He may establish His covenant which He sware unto thy fathers, as it is this day. *Deuteronomy 8:18*

Keep therefore the words of this covenant, and do them, that ye may prosper in all that ye do. *Deuteronomy 29:9*

Only be thou strong and very courageous, that thou mayest observe to do according to all the law, which Moses My servant commanded thee: turn not from it to the right hand or to the left, that thou mayest prosper whithersoever thou goest.

This book of the law shall not depart out of thy mouth; but thou shalt meditate therein day and night, that thou mayest observe to do according to all that is written therein: for then thou shalt make thy way prosperous, and then thou shalt have good success. *Joshua 1:7,8*

He becometh poor that dealeth with a slack hand: but the hand of the diligent maketh rich. *Proverbs 10:4*

The soul of the sluggard desireth, and hath nothing: but the soul of the diligent shall be made fat. *Proverbs 13:4*

He that tilleth his land shall have plenty of bread: but he that followeth after vain persons shall have poverty enough.

A faithful man shall abound with blessings: but he that maketh haste to be rich shall not be innocent.

Proverbs 28:19,20

Not slothful in business; fervent in spirit; serving the Lord; *Romans 12:11*

But this I say, He which soweth sparingly shall reap also sparingly; and he which soweth bountifully shall reap also bountifully. *2 Corinthians 9:6*

But my God shall supply all your need according to His riches in glory by Christ Jesus. *Philippians 4:19*

51

WHEN YOU WANT TO RETIRE

The Lord will give strength unto His people; the Lord will bless His people with peace. *Psalm 29:11*

Commit thy way unto the Lord; trust also in Him; and He shall bring it to pass.
Psalm 37:5

Rest in the Lord, and wait patiently for Him: fret not thyself because of him who prospereth in his way, because of the man who bringeth wicked devices to pass.
Psalm 37:7

My flesh and my heart faileth: but God is the strength of my heart, and my portion for ever. *Psalm 73:26*

I will hear what God the Lord will speak: for He will speak peace unto His people, and to His saints: but let them not turn again to folly. *Psalm 85:8*

Thou wilt keep him in perfect peace, whose mind is stayed on Thee: because he trusteth in Thee. *Isaiah 26:3*

To whom He said, This is the rest wherewith ye may cause the weary to rest; and this is the refreshing: yet they would not hear. *Isaiah 28:12*

For thus saith the Lord God, the Holy One of Israel; In returning and rest shall ye be saved; in quietness and in confidence shall be your strength: and ye would not.
Isaiah 30:15

Come unto Me, all ye that labour and are heavy laden, and I will give you rest.
Matthew 11:28

Take My yoke upon you, and learn of Me; for I am meek and lowly in heart: and ye shall find rest unto your souls.
Matthew 11:29

And He said unto them, Come ye yourselves apart into a desert place, and rest a while: for there were many coming and going, and they had no leisure so much as to eat. *Mark 6:31*

Peace I leave with you, My peace I give unto you: not as the world giveth, give I unto you. Let not your heart be troubled, neither let it be afraid. *John 14:27*

Know ye not that ye are the temple of God, and that the Spirit of God dwelleth in you? *1 Corinthians 3:16*

If any man defile the temple of God, him shall God destroy; for the temple of God is holy, which temple ye are. *1 Corinthians 3:17*

And let us not be weary in well doing: for in due season we shall reap, if we faint not. *Galatians 6:9*

Brethren, I count not myself to have apprehended: but this one thing I do, forgetting those things which are behind, and reaching forth unto those things which are before,

I press toward the mark for the prize of the high calling of God in Christ Jesus.
Philippians 3:13,14

But my God shall supply all your need according to His riches in glory by Christ Jesus. *Philippians 4:19*

Satan's Favorite Entry Point
Into Your Life
Is Always Through Someone
You Have Chosen
To Trust.

-MIKE MURDOCK

Copyright © 2001 by Mike Murdock • Wisdom International
The Wisdom Center • P.O. Box 99 • Denton, TX 76202

YOUR STRESS

~ 52 ~

WHEN YOU HAVE BEEN DECEIVED

Thou shalt destroy them that speak leasing: the Lord will abhor the bloody and deceitful man.   *Psalm 5:6*

But as for me, I will come into Thy house in the multitude of Thy mercy: and in Thy fear will I worship toward Thy holy temple.
Psalm 5:7

Into thine hand I commit my spirit: Thou hast redeemed me, O Lord God of truth.   *Psalm 31:5*

I have hated them that regard lying vanities: but I trust in the Lord.
Psalm 31:6

Let not them that are mine enemies

wrongfully rejoice over me: neither let them wink with the eye that hate me without a cause. *Psalm 35:19*

For they speak not peace: but they devise deceitful matters against them that are quiet in the land. *Psalm 35:20*

This thou hast seen, O Lord: keep not silence: O Lord, be not far from me.
Psalm 35:22

He only is my rock and my salvation; He is my defence; I shall not be greatly moved. *Psalm 62:2*

Trust in the Lord with all thine heart; and lean not unto thine own understanding.
Proverbs 3:5

In all thy ways acknowledge Him, and He shall direct thy paths. *Proverbs 3:6*

He that handleth a matter wisely shall find good: and whoso trusteth in the Lord, happy is he. *Proverbs 16:20*

A wicked man hardeneth his face: but as for the upright, he directeth his way.
Proverbs 21:29

He that is of a proud heart stirreth up strife: but he that putteth his trust in the Lord shall be made fat. *Proverbs 28:25*

The fear of man bringeth a snare: but whoso putteth his trust in the Lord shall be safe. *Proverbs 29:25*

Behold, God is my salvation; I will trust, and not be afraid: for the Lord Jehovah is my strength and my song; He also is become my salvation. *Isaiah 12:2*

Thou wilt keep him in perfect peace, whose mind is stayed on Thee: because he trusteth in Thee. *Isaiah 26:3*

O Lord, be gracious unto us; we have waited for Thee: be Thou their arm every morning, our salvation also in the time of trouble. *Isaiah 33:2*

Trust ye not in a friend, put ye not confidence in a guide: keep the doors of thy mouth from her that lieth in thy bosom.
Micah 7:5

For the son dishonoureth the father, the

daughter riseth up against her mother, the daughter in law against her mother in law; a man's enemies are the men of his own house. *Micah 7:6*

Therefore I will look unto the Lord; I will wait for the God of my salvation: my God will hear me. *Micah 7:7*

Wherefore putting away lying, speak every man truth with his neighbour: for we are members one of another.
Ephesians 4:25

Be ye angry, and sin not: let not the sun go down upon your wrath: *Ephesians 4:26*

Let all bitterness, and wrath, and anger, and clamour, and evil speaking, be put away from you, with all malice: *Ephesians 4:31*

Looking diligently lest any man fail of the grace of God; lest any root of bitterness springing up trouble you, and thereby many be defiled; *Hebrews 12:15*

~ 53 ~

WHEN YOU FEEL BETRAYED

For I have heard the slander of many: fear was on every side: while they took counsel together against me, they devised to take away my life. *Psalm 31:13*

My times are in Thy hand: deliver me from the hand of mine enemies, and from them that persecute me. *Psalm 31:15*

Make Thy face to shine upon Thy servant: save me for Thy mercies' sake.
Psalm 31:16

The angel of the Lord encampeth round about them that fear Him, and delivereth them. *Psalm 34:7*

Yea, mine own familiar friend, in whom I trusted, which did eat of my bread, hath lifted up his heel against me. *Psalm 41:9*

But Thou, O Lord, be merciful unto me,

and raise me up, that I may requite them.
Psalm 41:10

By this I know that Thou favourest me, because mine enemy doth not triumph over me. *Psalm 41:11*

In the day of my trouble I will call upon Thee: for Thou wilt answer me. *Psalm 86:7*

He shall cover thee with His feathers, and under His wings shalt thou trust: His truth shall be thy shield and buckler.
Psalm 91:4

Thou shalt not be afraid for the terror by night; nor for the arrow that flieth by day;
Psalm 91:5

For the Lord God will help me; therefore shall I not be confounded: therefore have I set my face like a flint, and I know that I shall not be ashamed. *Isaiah 50:7*

He is near that justifieth me; who will contend with me? let us stand together: who is mine adversary? let him come near to me.
Isaiah 50:8

Behold, the Lord God will help me; who is he that shall condemn me? lo, they all shall wax old as a garment; the moth shall eat them up. *Isaiah 50:9*

But I will deliver thee in that day, saith the Lord: and thou shalt not be given into the hand of the men of whom thou art afraid.
Jeremiah 39:17

For I will surely deliver thee, and thou shalt not fall by the sword, but thy life shall be for a prey unto thee: because thou hast put thy trust in Me, saith the Lord.
Jeremiah 39:18

Rejoice not against me, O mine enemy: when I fall, I shall arise; when I sit in darkness, the Lord shall be a light unto me.
Micah 7:8

Be ye angry, and sin not: let not the sun go down upon your wrath:
Ephesians 4:26

Let all bitterness, and wrath, and anger, and clamour, and evil speaking, be put away from you, with all malice: *Ephesians 4:31*

Your Own Seeds
Have Created
Your Present Harvest.

-MIKE MURDOCK

Copyright © 2001 by Mike Murdock • Wisdom International
The Wisdom Center • P.O. Box 99 • Denton, TX 76202

54

WHEN YOU EXPERIENCE JEALOUSY TOWARDS THE SUCCESS OF OTHERS

I will bless the Lord, Who hath given me counsel: my reins also instruct me in the night seasons. *Psalm 16:7*

I have set the Lord always before me: because He is at my right hand, I shall not be moved. *Psalm 16:8*

Therefore my heart is glad, and my glory rejoiceth: my flesh also shall rest in hope. *Psalm 16:9*

Behold, thou desirest truth in the inward parts: and in the hidden part Thou shalt make me to know Wisdom. *Psalm 51:6*

Purge me with hyssop, and I shall be clean: wash me, and I shall be whiter than snow. *Psalm 51:7*

Create in me a clean heart, O God; and renew a right spirit within me. *Psalm 51:10*

In God I will praise His word, in God I have put my trust; I will not fear what flesh can do unto me. *Psalm 56:4*

Teach me Thy way, O Lord; I will walk in Thy truth: unite my heart to fear Thy name. *Psalm 86:11*

For the Lord shall be thy confidence, and shall keep thy foot from being taken. *Proverbs 3:26*

Buy the truth, and sell it not; also wisdom, and instruction, and understanding. *Proverbs 23:23*

Behold, God is my salvation; I will trust, and not be afraid: for the Lord Jehovah is my strength and my song; He also is become my salvation. *Isaiah 12:2*

And thou, son of man, be not afraid of them, neither be afraid of their words, though briers and thorns be with thee, and thou dost dwell among scorpions: be not afraid of their words, nor be dismayed at their looks, though they be a rebellious house. *Ezekiel 2:6*

Doth not behave itself unseemly, seeketh not her own, is not easily provoked, thinketh no evil; *1 Corinthians 13:5*

For the weapons of our warfare are not carnal, but mighty through God to the pulling down of strong holds;
2 Corinthians 10:4

Casting down imaginations, and every high thing that exalteth itself against the knowledge of God, and bringing into captivity every thought to the obedience of Christ; *2 Corinthians 10:5*

Finally, my brethren, be strong in the Lord, and in the power of His might.
Ephesians 6:10

Finally, brethren, whatsoever things are true, whatsoever things are honest, whatsoever things are just, whatsoever things are pure, whatsoever things are lovely, whatsoever things are of good report; if there be any virtue, and if there be any praise, think on these things. *Philippians 4:8*

Quenched the violence of fire, escaped the edge of the sword, out of weakness were made strong, waxed valiant in fight, turned to flight the armies of the aliens. *Hebrews 11:34*

55

WHEN YOU FEEL USED

I have set the Lord always before me: because He is at my right hand, I shall not be moved.
Psalm 16:8

Therefore my heart is glad, and my glory rejoiceth: my flesh also shall rest in hope.
Psalm 16:9

Judge me, O Lord; for I have walked in mine integrity: I have trusted also in the Lord; therefore I shall not slide. *Psalm 26:1*

For Thy lovingkindness is before mine eyes: and I have walked in Thy truth.
Psalm 26:3

Behold, Thou desirest truth in the inward parts: and in the hidden part Thou shalt make me to know wisdom. *Psalm 51:6*

For my love they are my adversaries: but I give myself unto prayer. *Psalm 109:4*

The wicked flee when no man pursueth: but the righteous are bold as a lion.
Proverbs 28:1

And His name through faith in His name hath made this man strong, whom ye see and know: yea, the faith which is by Him hath given him this perfect soundness in the presence of you all. *Acts 3:16*

Let love be without dissimulation, Abhor that which is evil; cleave to that which is good. *Romans 12:9*

Be kindly affectioned one to another with brotherly love; in honour preferring one another; *Romans 12:10*

Watch ye, stand fast in the faith, quit you like men, be strong. *1 Corinthians 16:13*

For the weapons of our warfare are not carnal, but mighty through God to the pulling down of strong holds;
2 Corinthians 10:4

Casting down imaginations, and every high thing that exalteth itself against the knowledge of God, and bringing into captivity every thought to the obedience of Christ; *2 Corinthians 10:5*

Wherefore putting away lying, speak every man truth with his neighbour: for we are members one of another. *Ephesians 4:25*

Be ye angry, and sin not: let not the sun go down upon your wrath:
Ephesians 4:26

Let all bitterness, and wrath, and anger, and clamour, and evil speaking, be put away from you, with all malice: *Ephesians 4:31*

Be careful for nothing; but in every thing by prayer and supplication with thanksgiving let your requests be made known unto God. *Philippians 4:6*

And the peace of God, which passeth all understanding, shall keep your hearts and minds through Christ Jesus.
Philippians 4:7

I can do all things through Christ which strengtheneth me. *Philippians 4:13*

Thou therefore, my son, be strong in the grace that is in Christ Jesus. *2 Timothy 2:1*

Looking diligently lest any man fail of the grace of God; lest any root of bitterness springing up trouble you, and thereby many be defiled; *Hebrews 12:15*

~ 56 ~

WHEN YOU FACE LITIGATION

But there is a spirit in man: and the inspiration of the Almighty giveth them understanding. *Job 32:8*

I will bless the Lord, Who hath given me counsel: my reins also instruct me in the night seasons. *Psalm 16:7*

The secret of the Lord is with them that fear Him; and He will shew them His covenant. *Psalm 25:14*

I will instruct thee and teach thee in the way which thou shalt go: I will guide thee with Mine eye. *Psalm 32:8*

Commit thy way unto the Lord; trust also in Him; and He shall bring it to pass.
Psalm 37:5

Rest in the Lord, and wait patiently for Him: fret not thyself because of him who

prospereth in his way, because of the man who bringeth wicked devices to pass.
Psalm 37:7

Cease from anger, and forsake wrath: fret not thyself in any wise to do evil.
Psalm 37:8

Behold, Thou desirest truth in the inward parts: and in the hidden part Thou shalt make me to know wisdom. *Psalm 51:6*

Unto the upright there ariseth light in the darkness: He is gracious, and full of compassion, and righteous. *Psalm 112:4*

He layeth up sound wisdom for the righteous: He is a buckler to them that walk uprightly. *Proverbs 2:7*

Trust in the Lord with all thine heart; and lean not unto thine own understanding.
Proverbs 3:5

In all thy ways acknowledge Him, and He shall direct thy paths. *Proverbs 3:6*

And thine ears shall hear a word behind thee, saying, This is the way, walk ye in it, when ye turn to the right hand, and when ye turn to the left. *Isaiah 30:21*

Fear thou not; for I am with thee: be not dismayed; for I am thy God: I will strengthen thee; yea, I will help thee; yea, I will uphold thee with the right hand of My righteousness. *Isaiah 41:10*

And I will bring the blind by a way that they knew not; I will lead them in paths that they have not known: I will make darkness light before them, and crooked things straight. These things will I do unto them, and not forsake them. *Isaiah 42:16*

Thus saith the Lord, thy Redeemer, the Holy One of Israel; I am the Lord thy God which teacheth thee to profit, which leadeth thee by the way that thou shouldest go.
Isaiah 48:17

I thank Thee, and praise Thee, O Thou God of my fathers, who hast given me wisdom and might, and hast made known unto me now what we desired of Thee: for Thou hast now made known unto us the king's matter. *Daniel 2:23*

And when they bring you unto the synagogues, and unto magistrates, and powers, take ye no thought how or what thing ye shall answer, or what ye shall say:
Luke 12:11

For the Holy Ghost shall teach you in the same hour what ye ought to say.
Luke 12:12

For I will give you a mouth and wisdom, which all your adversaries shall not be able to gainsay nor resist. *Luke 21:15*

Howbeit when He, the Spirit of truth, is come, He will guide you into all truth: for He shall not speak of Himself; but whatsoever He shall hear, that shall He speak: and He will shew you things to come.
John 16:13

He shall glorify Me: for He shall receive of Mine, and shall shew it unto you.
John 16:14

For God hath not given us the spirit of fear; but of power, and of love, and of a sound mind. *2 Timothy 1:7*

57

WHEN TRAGEDY STRIKES

Thou, which hast shewed me great and sore troubles, shalt quicken me again, and shalt bring me up again from the depths of the earth. *Psalm 71:20*

My flesh and my heart faileth: but God is the strength of my heart, and my portion for ever. *Psalm 73:26*

It is good for me that I have been afflicted; that I might learn thy statutes. *Psalm 119:71*

Though I walk in the midst of trouble, Thou wilt revive me: Thou shalt stretch forth Thine hand against the wrath of mine enemies, and Thy right hand shall save me. *Psalm 138:7*

The Lord will perfect that which concerneth me: Thy mercy, O Lord, endureth for ever: forsake not the works of Thine own hands. *Psalm 138:8*

If thou faint in the day of adversity, thy strength is small. *Proverbs 24:10*

In the day of prosperity be joyful, but in the day of adversity consider: God also hath set the one over against the other, to the end that man should find nothing after him. *Ecclesiastes 7:14*

When thou passest through the waters, I will be with thee; and through the rivers, they shall not overflow thee: when thou walkest through the fire, thou shalt not be burned; neither shall the flame kindle upon thee. *Isaiah 43:2*

The Lord is good, a strong hold in the day of trouble; and He knoweth them that trust in Him. *Nahum 1:7*

We are troubled on every side, yet not distressed; we are perplexed, but not in despair; *2 Corinthians 4:8*

Persecuted, but not forsaken; cast down, but not destroyed; *2 Corinthians 4:9*

Looking unto Jesus the author and finisher of our faith; Who for the joy that was set before Him endured the cross, despising the shame, and is set down at the right hand of the throne of God. *Hebrews 12:2*

For even hereunto were ye called: because Christ also suffered for us, leaving us an example, that ye should follow His steps: *1 Peter 2:21*

Who, when He was reviled, reviled not again; when He suffered, He threatened not; but committed Himself to Him that judgeth righteously: *1 Peter 2:23*

Beloved, think it not strange concerning the fiery trial which is to try you, as though some strange thing happened unto you:
1 Peter 4:12

But rejoice, inasmuch as ye are partakers of Christ's sufferings; that, when His glory shall be revealed, ye may be glad also with exceeding joy. *1 Peter 4:13*

Casting all your care upon Him; for He careth for you. *1 Peter 5:7*

Whom resist stedfast in the faith, knowing that the same afflictions are accomplished in your brethren that are in the world. *1 Peter 5:9*

Fear none of those things which thou shalt suffer: behold, the devil shall cast some of you into prison, that ye may be tried; and ye shall have tribulation ten days: be thou faithful unto death, and I will give thee a crown of life. *Revelation 2:10*

～58～

WHEN YOU FEEL OVERWORKED

I will both lay me down in peace, and sleep: for Thou, Lord, only makest me dwell in safety. *Psalm 4:8*

He maketh me to lie down in green pastures: He leadeth me beside the still waters. *Psalm 23:2*

He restoreth my soul: He leadeth me in the paths of righteousness for His name's sake. *Psalm 23:3*

When Thou saidst, Seek ye My face; my heart said unto Thee, Thy face, Lord, will I seek. *Psalm 27:8*

The Lord will give strength unto His people; the Lord will bless His people with peace. *Psalm 29:11*

Commit thy way unto the Lord; trust also in Him; and He shall bring it to pass.
Psalm 37:5

Rest in the Lord, and wait patiently for Him: fret not thyself because of him who prospereth in his way, because of the man who bringeth wicked devices to pass.
Psalm 37:7

My flesh and my heart faileth: but God is the strength of my heart, and my portion for ever.
Psalm 73:26

I will hear what God the Lord will speak: for He will speak peace unto His people, and to His saints: but let them not turn again to folly.
Psalm 85:8

Thou wilt keep him in perfect peace, whose mind is stayed on Thee: because he trusteth in Thee.
Isaiah 26:3

To whom He said, This is the rest wherewith ye may cause the weary to rest; and this is the refreshing: yet they would not hear.
Isaiah 28:12

For thus saith the Lord God, the Holy One of Israel; In returning and rest shall ye be saved; in quietness and in confidence shall be your strength: and ye would not.
Isaiah 30:15

Come unto Me, all ye that labour and are heavy laden, and I will give you rest.
Matthew 11:28

Take My yoke upon you, and learn of Me; for I am meek and lowly in heart: and ye shall find rest unto your souls.
Matthew 11:29

And He said unto them, Come ye yourselves apart into a desert place, and rest a while: for there were many coming and going, and they had no leisure so much as to eat. *Mark 6:31*

Peace I leave with you, My peace I give unto you: not as the world giveth, give I unto you. Let not your heart be troubled, neither let it be afraid. *John 14:27*

Know ye not that ye are the temple of God, and that the Spirit of God dwelleth in you? *1 Corinthians 3:16*

Never Pursue Anything Incapable Of Motivating You.

-MIKE MURDOCK

Copyright © 2001 by Mike Murdock • Wisdom International
The Wisdom Center • P.O. Box 99 • Denton, TX 76202

59

WHEN YOU EXPERIENCE BURNOUT AND LOSS OF INTEREST

But Thou, O Lord, art a shield for me; my glory, and the lifter up of mine head.
Psalm 3:3

My voice shalt Thou hear in the morning, O Lord; in the morning will I direct my prayer unto Thee, and will look up.
Psalm 5:3

For the Lord shall be thy confidence, and shall keep thy foot from being taken.
Proverbs 3:26

Let thine eyes look right on, and let thine eyelids look straight before thee.
Proverbs 4:25

In the fear of the Lord is strong confidence: and His children shall have a place of refuge. *Proverbs 14:26*

He giveth power to the faint; and to them that have no might He increaseth strength. *Isaiah 40:29*

But they that wait upon the Lord shall renew their strength; they shall mount up with wings as eagles; they shall run, and not be weary; and they shall walk, and not faint. *Isaiah 40:31*

Fear thou not; for I am with thee: be not dismayed; for I am thy God: I will strengthen thee; yea, I will help thee; yea, I will uphold thee with the right hand of My righteousness. *Isaiah 41:10*

When thou passest through the waters, I will be with thee; and through the rivers, they shall not overflow thee: when thou walkest through the fire, thou shalt not be burned; neither shall the flame kindle upon thee. *Isaiah 43:2*

Then he answered and spake unto me, saying, This is the word of the Lord unto Zerubbabel, saying, Not by might, nor by power, but by My spirit, saith the Lord of hosts. *Zechariah 4:6*

~ 60 ~

WHEN YOU FEEL THREATENED

Happy art thou, O Israel: who is like unto thee, O people saved by the Lord, the shield of thy help, and Who is the sword of thy excellency! And thine enemies shall be found liars unto thee; and thou shalt tread upon their high places.   *Deuteronomy 33:29*

And he said, The Lord is my rock, and my fortress, and my deliverer;
2 Samuel 22:2

Lord, how are they increased that trouble me! many are they that rise up against me.   *Psalm 3:1*

But Thou, O Lord, art a shield for me; my glory, and the lifter up of mine head.
Psalm 3:3

In my distress I called upon the Lord, and cried unto my God: He heard my voice out of His temple, and my cry came before Him, even into His ears.   *Psalm 18:6*

Thou hast also given me the shield of thy salvation: and Thy right hand hath holden me up, and Thy gentleness hath made me great. *Psalm 18:35*

The Lord is my strength and my shield; my heart trusted in Him, and I am helped: therefore my heart greatly rejoiceth; and with my song will I praise Him. *Psalm 28:7*

The angel of the Lord encampeth round about them that fear Him, and delivereth them. *Psalm 34:7*

What time I am afraid, I will trust in Thee. *Psalm 56:3*

In God I will praise His word, in God I have put my trust; I will not fear what flesh can do unto me. *Psalm 56:4*

For the Lord God is a sun and shield: the Lord will give grace and glory: no good thing will He withhold from them that walk uprightly. *Psalm 84:11*

He shall cover thee with His feathers, and under His wings shalt thou trust: His truth shall be thy shield and buckler.
Psalm 91:4

Ye that fear the Lord, trust in the Lord: He is their help and their shield.
Psalm 115:11

Thou art my hiding place and my shield: I hope in Thy word. *Psalm 119:114*

My goodness, and my fortress; my high tower, and my deliverer; my shield, and He in whom I trust; who subdueth my people under me. *Psalm 144:2*

Fear thou not; for I am with thee: be not dismayed; for I am thy God: I will strengthen thee; yea, I will help thee; yea, I will uphold thee with the right hand of My righteousness. *Isaiah 41:10*

For I the Lord thy God will hold thy right hand, saying unto thee, Fear not; I will help thee. *Isaiah 41:13*

Above all, taking the shield of faith, Wherewith ye shall be able to quench all the fiery darts of the wicked. *Ephesians 6:16*

Crisis Is
The School Of Discovery.

-MIKE MURDOCK

Copyright © 2001 by Mike Murdock • Wisdom International
The Wisdom Center • P.O. Box 99 • Denton, TX 76202

61

WHEN YOU FEEL LIKE GIVING UP

Wait on the Lord: be of good courage, and He shall strengthen thine heart: wait, I say, on the Lord. *Psalm 27:14*

Be of good courage, and He shall strengthen your heart, all ye that hope in the Lord. *Psalm 31:24*

For in Thee, O Lord, do I hope: Thou wilt hear, O Lord my God. *Psalm 38:15*

And now, Lord, what wait I for? my hope is in Thee. *Psalm 39:7*

But I will hope continually, and will yet praise Thee more and more. *Psalm 71:14*

Happy is he that hath the God of Jacob for his help, whose hope is in the Lord his God: *Psalm 146:5*

Trust in the Lord with all thine heart; and lean not unto thine own understanding.
Proverbs 3:5

Hope deferred maketh the heart sick: but when the desire cometh, it is a tree of life.
Proverbs 13:12

So shall the knowledge of wisdom be unto thy soul: when thou hast found it, then there shall be a reward, and thy expectation shall not be cut off.
Proverbs 24:14

Blessed is the man that trusteth in the Lord, and whose hope the Lord is.
Jeremiah 17:7

It is good that a man should both hope and quietly wait for the salvation of the Lord.
Lamentations 3:26

Jesus said unto him, If thou canst believe, all things are possible to him that believeth.
Mark 9:23

And straightway the father of the child cried out, and said with tears, Lord, I believe; help Thou mine unbelief.
Mark 9:24

Therefore I say unto you, What things soever ye desire, when ye pray, believe that ye receive them, and ye shall have them.
Mark 11:24

But if we hope for that we see not, then do we with patience wait for it.
Romans 8:25

Rejoicing in hope; patient in tribulation; continuing instant in prayer;
Romans 12:12

Now the God of hope fill you with all joy and peace in believing, that ye may abound in hope, through the power of the Holy Ghost. *Romans 15:13*

Now faith is the substance of things hoped for, the evidence of things not seen.
Hebrews 11:1

62

WHEN YOU DO NOT FEEL GOD'S PRESENCE

And he went out to meet Asa, and said unto him, Hear ye me, Asa, and all Judah and Benjamin; The Lord is with you, while ye be with Him; and if ye seek Him, He will be found of you; but if ye forsake Him, He will forsake you. *2 Chronicles 15:2*

For I was envious at the foolish, when I saw the prosperity of the wicked.
Psalm 73:3

When I thought to know this, it was too painful for me; *Psalm 73:16*

Until I went into the sanctuary of God; then understood I their end. *Psalm 73:17*

But it is good for me to draw near to God: I have put my trust in the Lord God, that I may declare all Thy works.
Psalm 73:28

The Lord is nigh unto all them that call upon Him, to all that call upon Him in truth.
Psalm 145:18

Seek ye the Lord while He may be found, call ye upon Him while He is near:
Isaiah 55:6

They shall enter into My sanctuary, and they shall come near to My table, to minister unto Me, and they shall keep My charge.
Ezekiel 44:16

But seek ye first the kingdom of God, and His righteousness; and all these things shall be added unto you. *Matthew 6:33*

This people draweth nigh unto Me with their mouth, and honoureth Me with their lips; but their heart is far from Me.
Matthew 15:8

And the cares of this world, and the deceitfulness of riches, and the lusts of other things entering in, choke the word, and it becometh unfruitful. *Mark 4:19*

And that which fell among thorns are

they, which, when they have heard, go forth, and are choked with cares and riches and pleasures of this life, and bring no fruit to perfection. *Luke 8:14*

And take heed to yourselves, lest at any time your hearts be overcharged with surfeiting, and drunkenness, and cares of this life, and so that day come upon you unawares. *Luke 21:34*

Ye did run well; who did hinder you that ye should not obey the truth? *Galatians 5:7*

Neglect not the gift that is in thee, which was given thee by prophecy, with the laying on of the hands of the presbytery.
1 Timothy 4:14

How shall we escape, if we neglect so great salvation; which at the first began to be spoken by the Lord, and was confirmed unto us by them that heard Him;
Hebrews 2:3

Let us hold fast the profession of our faith without wavering; for He is faithful that promised; *Hebrews 10:23*

Not forsaking the assembling of ourselves together, as the manner of some is; but exhorting one another: and so much the more, as ye see the day approaching.
Hebrews 10:25

Looking unto Jesus the author and finisher of our faith; Who for the joy that was set before Him endured the cross, despising the shame, and is set down at the right hand of the throne of God. *Hebrews 12:2*

Draw nigh to God, and He will draw nigh to you. Cleanse your hands, ye sinners; and purify your hearts, ye double minded.
James 4:8

63

WHEN YOU HAVE BAD MEMORIES OF THE PAST

The eternal God is thy refuge, and underneath are the everlasting arms: and He shall thrust out the enemy from before thee; and shall say, Destroy them.
Deuteronomy 33:27

And they that know Thy name will put their trust in Thee: for Thou, Lord, hast not forsaken them that seek Thee. *Psalm 9:10*

Yea, though I walk through the valley of the shadow of death, I will fear no evil: for Thou art with me; Thy rod and Thy staff they comfort me. *Psalm 23:4*

I have been young, and now am old; yet have I not seen the righteous forsaken, nor His seed begging bread. *Psalm 37:25*

For the Lord loveth judgment, and

forsaketh not His saints; they are preserved for ever: but the seed of the wicked shall be cut off. *Psalm 37:28*

Save me, O God; for the waters are come in unto my soul. *Psalm 69:1*

I sink in deep mire, where there is no standing: I am come into deep waters, where the floods overflow me. *Psalm 69:2*

I am weary of my crying: my throat is dried: mine eyes fail while I wait for my God. *Psalm 69:3*

He healeth the broken in heart, and bindeth up their wounds. *Psalm 147:3*

For Thou hast been a strength to the poor, a strength to the needy in his distress, a refuge from the storm, a shadow from the heat, when the blast of the terrible ones is as a storm against the wall. *Isaiah 25:4*

He giveth power to the faint; and to them that have no might He increaseth strength. *Isaiah 40:29*

Fear thou not; for I am with thee: be

not dismayed; for I am thy God: I will strengthen thee; yea, I will help thee; yea, I will uphold thee with the right hand of My righteousness. *Isaiah 41:10*

But the very hairs of your head are all numbered. *Matthew 10:30*

And I will pray the Father, and he shall give you another Comforter, that He may abide with you for ever; *John 14:16*

Even the Spirit of truth; Whom the world cannot receive, because it seeth Him not, neither knoweth Him: but ye know Him; for He dwelleth with you, and shall be in you.
John 14:17

I will not leave you comfortless: I will come to you. *John 14:18*

At my first answer no man stood with me, but all men forsook me: I pray God that it may not be laid to their charge.
2 Timothy 4:16

Notwithstanding the Lord stood with me, and strengthened me; that by me the

preaching might be fully known, and that all the Gentiles might hear: and I was delivered out of the mouth of the lion.
2 Timothy 4:17

And the Lord shall deliver me from every evil work, and will preserve me unto His heavenly kingdom: to Whom be glory for ever and ever. Amen.   *2 Timothy 4:18*

Let us therefore come boldly unto the throne of grace, that we may obtain mercy, and find grace to help in time of need.
Hebrews 4:16

Let your conversation be without covetousness; and be content with such things as ye have: for He hath said, I will never leave thee, nor forsake thee.
Hebrews 13:5

64

WHEN SLANDEROUS REMARKS CIRCULATE YOUR OFFICE

Keep thy tongue from evil, and thy lips from speaking guile. *Psalm 34:13*

The mouth of the righteous speaketh wisdom, and his tongue talketh of judgment. *Psalm 37:30*

I said, I will take heed to my ways, that I sin not with my tongue: I will keep my mouth with a bridle, while the wicked is before me. *Psalm 39:1*

Whoso offereth praise glorifieth Me: and to him that ordereth his conversation aright will I shew the salvation of God. *Psalm 50:23*

But God shall shoot at them with an arrow; suddenly shall they be wounded. *Psalm 64:7*

Princes also did sit and speak against me: but thy servant did meditate in thy statutes. *Psalm 119:23*

Set a watch, O Lord, before my mouth; keep the door of my lips. *Psalm 141:3*

In the multitude of words there wanteth not sin: but he that refraineth his lips is wise. *Proverbs 10:19*

The lip of truth shall be established for ever: but a lying tongue is but for a moment.
Proverbs 12:19

He that keepeth his mouth keepeth his life: but he that openeth wide his lips shall have destruction. *Proverbs 13:3*

A soft answer turneth away wrath: but grievous words stir up anger.
Proverbs 15:1

The heart of the righteous studieth to answer: but the mouth of the wicked poureth out evil things. *Proverbs 15:28*

A fool uttereth all his mind: but a wise man keepeth it in till afterwards.
Proverbs 29:11

Seest thou a man that is hasty in his words? there is more hope of a fool than of him. *Proverbs 29:20*

A good man out of the good treasure of the heart bringeth forth good things: and an evil man out of the evil treasure bringeth forth evil things. *Matthew 12:35*

Let no corrupt communication proceed out of your mouth, but that which is good to the use of edifying, that it may minister grace unto the hearers. *Ephesians 4:29*

Let all bitterness, and wrath, and anger, and clamour, and evil speaking, be put away from you, with all malice: *Ephesians 4:31*

Not rendering evil for evil, or railing for railing: but contrariwise blessing; knowing that ye are thereunto called, that ye should inherit a blessing. *1 Peter 3:9*

For he that will love life, and see good days, let him refrain his tongue from evil, and his lips that they speak no guile:
1 Peter 3:10

Your Wisdom

~ 65 ~

Achievement

Have not I commanded thee? Be strong and of a good courage; be not afraid, neither be thou dismayed: for the Lord thy God is with thee whithersoever thou goest.
Joshua 1:9

Be ye strong therefore, and let not your hands be weak: for your work shall be rewarded. *2 Chronicles 15:7*

A good man sheweth favour, and lendeth: he will guide his affairs with discretion. *Psalm 112:5*

Surely he shall not be moved for ever: the righteous shall be in everlasting remembrance. *Psalm 112:6*

He shall not be afraid of evil tidings: his heart is fixed, trusting in the Lord.
Psalm 112:7

Blessed is the man that trusteth in the Lord, and whose hope the Lord is.
Jeremiah 17:7

Jesus said unto him, If thou canst believe, all things are possible to him that believeth. *Mark 9:23*

And the Lord said, If ye had faith as a grain of mustard seed, ye might say unto this sycamine tree, Be thou plucked up by the root, and be thou planted in the sea; and it should obey you. *Luke 17:6*

And not only so, but we glory in tribulations also: knowing that tribulation worketh patience; *Romans 5:3*

And patience, experience; and experience, hope: *Romans 5:4*

And hope maketh not ashamed; because the love of God is shed abroad in our hearts by the Holy Ghost which is given unto us.
Romans 5:5

I can do all things through Christ which strengtheneth me. *Philippians 4:13*

Cast not away therefore your confidence, which hath great recompence of reward. *Hebrews 10:35*

66

AMBITION

He becometh poor that dealeth with a slack hand: but the hand of the diligent maketh rich. *Proverbs 10:4*

The thoughts of the diligent tend only to plenteousness; but of every one that is hasty only to want. *Proverbs 21:5*

Seest thou a man diligent in his business? he shall stand before kings; he shall not stand before mean men.
Proverbs 22:29

Be thou diligent to know the state of thy flocks, and look well to thy herds.
Proverbs 27:23

Whatsoever thy hand findeth to do, do it with thy might; for there is no work, nor device, nor knowledge, nor wisdom, in the grave, whither thou goest. *Ecclesiastes 9:10*

Let your light so shine before men, that they may see your good works, and glorify your Father which is in heaven.
Matthew 5:16

But seek ye first the kingdom of God, and His righteousness; and all these things shall be added unto you.   *Matthew 6:33*

And that servant, which knew his lord's will, and prepared not himself, neither did according to his will, shall be beaten with many stripes.   *Luke 12:47*

Strive to enter in at the strait gate: for many, I say unto you, will seek to enter in, and shall not be able.   *Luke 13:24*

And every man that striveth for the mastery is temperate in all things. Now they do it to obtain a corruptible crown; but we an incorruptible.   *1 Corinthians 9:25*

I press toward the mark for the prize of the high calling of God in Christ Jesus.
Philippians 3:14

Charge them that are rich in this world,

that they be not highminded, nor trust in uncertain riches, but in the living God, who giveth us richly all things to enjoy;
1 Timothy 6:17

Study to shew thyself approved unto God, a workman that needeth not to be ashamed, rightly dividing the word of truth.
2 Timothy 2:15

For God is not unrighteous to forget your work and labour of love, which ye have shewed toward His name, in that ye have ministered to the saints, and do minister.
Hebrews 6:10

Therefore to him that knoweth to do good, and doeth it not, to him it is sin.
James 4:17

～ 67 ～

ANGER

I will both lay me down in peace, and sleep: for Thou, Lord, only makest me dwell in safety. *Psalm 4:8*

Delight thyself also in the Lord; and He shall give thee the desires of thine heart.
Psalm 37:4

Commit thy way unto the Lord; trust also in Him; and He shall bring it to pass.
Psalm 37:5

Rest in the Lord, and wait patiently for Him: fret not thyself because of him who prospereth in his way, because of the man who bringeth wicked devices to pass.
Psalm 37:7

Cease from anger, and forsake wrath: fret not thyself in any wise to do evil.
Psalm 37:8

Great peace have they which love Thy

law: and nothing shall offend them.
Psalm 119:165

He that is slow to anger is better than the mighty; and he that ruleth his spirit than he that taketh a city. *Proverbs 16:32*

The discretion of a man deferreth his anger; and it is his glory to pass over a transgression. *Proverbs 19:11*

Better is the end of a thing than the beginning thereof: and the patient in spirit is better than the proud in spirit.
Ecclesiastes 7:8

Be not hasty in thy spirit to be angry: for anger resteth in the bosom of fools.
Ecclesiastes 7:9

Thou wilt keep him in perfect peace, whose mind is stayed on Thee: because he trusteth in Thee. *Isaiah 26:3*

Trust ye in the Lord for ever: for in the Lord Jehovah is everlasting strength:
Isaiah 26:4

Blessed are the peacemakers: for they shall be called the children of God.
Matthew 5:9

Peace I leave with you, My peace I give unto you: not as the world giveth, give I unto you. Let not your heart be troubled, neither let it be afraid. *John 14:27*

But the fruit of the Spirit is love, joy, peace, longsuffering, gentleness, goodness, faith, *Galatians 5:22*

Meekness, temperance: against such there is no law. *Galatians 5:23*

Be ye angry, and sin not: let not the sun go down upon your wrath: *Ephesians 4:26*

Do all things without murmurings and disputings: *Philippians 2:14*

I will therefore that men pray every where, lifting up holy hands, without wrath and doubting. *1 Timothy 2:8*

Wherefore, my beloved brethren, let every man be swift to hear, slow to speak, slow to wrath: *James 1:19*

Wherefore lay apart all filthiness and superfluity of naughtiness, and receive with meekness the engrafted word, which is able to save your souls. *James 1:21*

68

COMFORT

The eternal God is thy refuge, and underneath are the everlasting arms: and He shall thrust out the enemy from before thee; and shall say, Destroy them.
Deuteronomy 33:27

And David was greatly distressed; for the people spake of stoning him, because the soul of all the people was grieved, every man for his sons and for his daughters: but David encouraged himself in the Lord his God.
1 Samuel 30:6

Yea, though I walk through the valley of the shadow of death, I will fear no evil: for Thou art with me; Thy rod and Thy staff they comfort me. *Psalm 23:4*

For in the time of trouble He shall hide me in His pavilion: in the secret of His tabernacle shall He hide me; He shall set me up upon a rock.

And now shall mine head be lifted up

above mine enemies round about me: therefore will I offer in His tabernacle sacrifices of joy; I will sing, yea, I will sing praises unto the Lord. *Psalm 27:5,6*

For His anger endureth but a moment; in His favour is life: weeping may endure for a night, but joy cometh in the morning.
Psalm 30:5

I will be glad and rejoice in Thy mercy: for Thou hast considered my trouble; Thou hast known my soul in adversities.
Psalm 31:7

Cast thy burden upon the Lord, and He shall sustain thee: He shall never suffer the righteous to be moved. *Psalm 55:22*

Thou tellest my wanderings: put Thou my tears into Thy bottle: are they not in Thy book?

When I cry unto Thee, then shall mine enemies turn back: this I know; for God is for me.

In God will I praise His word: in the Lord will I praise His word. *Psalm 56:8-10*

This is my comfort in my affliction: for Thy word hath quickened me. *Psalm 119:50*

I remembered Thy judgments of old, O Lord; and have comforted myself.
Psalm 119:52

Thy statutes have been my songs in the house of my pilgrimage.   *Psalm 119:54*

And I will pray the Father, and He shall give you another Comforter, that He may abide with you for ever;

Even the Spirit of truth; Whom the world cannot receive, because it seeth Him not, neither knoweth Him: but ye know Him; for He dwelleth with you, and shall be in you.

I will not leave you comfortless: I will come to you.   *John 14:16-18*

But the Comforter, which is the Holy Ghost, Whom the Father will send in My name, He shall teach you all things, and bring all things to your remembrance, whatsoever I have said unto you.   *John 14:26*

Nevertheless I tell you the truth; It is expedient for you that I go away: for if I go not away, the Comforter will not come unto you; but if I depart, I will send Him unto you.   *John 16:7*

For he that speaketh in an unknown

tongue speaketh not unto men, but unto God: for no man understandeth him; howbeit in the spirit he speaketh mysteries.

But he that prophesieth speaketh unto men to edification, and exhortation, and comfort. *1 Corinthians 14:2,3*

Blessed be God, even the Father of our Lord Jesus Christ, the Father of mercies, and the God of all comfort;
Who comforteth us in all our tribulation, that we may be able to comfort them which are in any trouble, by the comfort wherewith we ourselves are comforted of God.
For as the sufferings of Christ abound in us, so our consolation also aboundeth by Christ. *2 Corinthians 1:3-5*

Wherefore comfort yourselves together, and edify one another, even as also ye do.
1 Thessalonians 5:11

But ye, beloved, building up yourselves on your most holy faith, praying in the Holy Ghost, *Jude 1:20*

69

COMMITMENT

Into thine hand I commit my spirit: Thou hast redeemed me, O Lord God of truth. *Psalm 31:5*

Commit thy way unto the Lord; trust also in Him; and He shall bring it to pass. *Psalm 37:5*

Blessed are they that keep His testimonies, and that seek Him with the whole heart. *Psalm 119:2*

Teach me to do Thy will; for Thou art my God: Thy Spirit is good; lead me into the land of uprightness. *Psalm 143:10*

And ye shall seek Me, and find Me, when ye shall search for Me with all your heart. *Jeremiah 29:13*

Jesus said unto him, Thou shalt love the Lord thy God with all thy heart, and with

all thy soul, and with all thy mind.
Matthew 22:37

If any man come to Me, and hate not his father, and mother, and wife, and children, and brethren, and sisters, yea, and his own life also, he cannot be My disciple.
Luke 14:26

And whosoever doth not bear his cross, and come after Me, cannot be My disciple.
Luke 14:27

So likewise, whosoever he be of you that forsaketh not all that he hath, he cannot be My disciple. *Luke 14:33*

And He said unto them, Verily I say unto you, There is no man that hath left house, or parents, or brethren, or wife, or children, for the kingdom of God's sake,
Luke 18:29

Who shall not receive manifold more in this present time, and in the world to come life everlasting. *Luke 18:30*

I beseech you therefore, brethren, by the mercies of God, that ye present your bodies

a living sacrifice, holy, acceptable unto God, which is your reasonable service.
Romans 12:1

And be not conformed to this world: but be ye transformed by the renewing of your mind, that ye may prove what is that good, and acceptable, and perfect, will of God.
Romans 12:2

I am crucified with Christ: nevertheless I live; yet not I, but Christ liveth in me: and the life which I now live in the flesh I live by the faith of the Son of God, who loved me, and gave Himself for me.   *Galatians 2:20*

🙞 70 🙜

COMPROMISING

Beware that thou forget not the Lord thy God, in not keeping His commandments, and His judgments, and His statutes, which I command thee this day: *Deuteronomy 8:11*

My son, if sinners entice thee, consent thou not. *Proverbs 1:10*

Discretion shall preserve thee, understanding shall keep thee:
Proverbs 2:11

Enter not into the path of the wicked, and go not in the way of evil men.
Proverbs 4:14

Avoid it, pass not by it, turn from it, and pass away. *Proverbs 4:15*

Cease, my son, to hear the instruction that causeth to err from the words of knowledge. *Proverbs 19:27*

He that walketh righteously, and speaketh uprightly; he that despiseth the gain of oppressions, that shaketh his hands from holding of bribes, that stoppeth his ears from hearing of blood, and shutteth his eyes from seeing evil; *Isaiah 33:15*

He shall dwell on high: his place of defence shall be the munitions of rocks: bread shall be given him; his waters shall be sure. *Isaiah 33:16*

He also that received seed among the thorns is he that heareth the word; and the care of this world, and the deceitfulness of riches, choke the word, and he becometh unfruitful. *Matthew 13:22*

Wherefore if thy hand or thy foot offend thee, cut them off, and cast them from thee: it is better for thee to enter into life halt or maimed, rather than having two hands or two feet to be cast into everlasting fire.
Matthew 18:8

Watch and pray, that ye enter not into temptation: the spirit indeed is willing, but the flesh is weak. *Matthew 26:41*

Let not sin therefore reign in your

mortal body, that ye should obey it in the lusts thereof. *Romans 6:12*

For sin shall not have dominion over you: for ye are not under the law, but under grace. *Romans 6:14*

Be not overcome of evil, but overcome evil with good. *Romans 12:21*

There hath no temptation taken you but such as is common to man: but God is faithful, who will not suffer you to be tempted above that ye are able; but will with the temptation also make a way to escape, that ye may be able to bear it.
1 Corinthians 10:13

Put on the whole armour of God, that ye may be able to stand against the wiles of the devil. *Ephesians 6:11*

For in that He Himself hath suffered being tempted, He is able to succour them that are tempted. *Hebrews 2:18*

For we have not an high priest which cannot be touched with the feeling of our infirmities; but was in all points tempted like as we are, yet without sin. *Hebrews 4:15*

Those Who Have Something
You Do Not Have
Know Something
You Do Not Know.

—MIKE MURDOCK

Copyright © 2001 by Mike Murdock • Wisdom International
The Wisdom Center • P.O. Box 99 • Denton, TX 76202

71

COUNSEL

Blessed is the man that walketh not in the counsel of the ungodly, nor standeth in the way of sinners, nor sitteth in the seat of the scornful. *Psalm 1:1*

Shew me Thy ways, O Lord; teach me Thy paths. *Psalm 25:4*

I will instruct thee and teach thee in the way which thou shalt go: I will guide thee with Mine eye. *Psalm 32:8*

Behold, thou desirest truth in the inward parts: and in the hidden part thou shalt make me to know wisdom. *Psalm 51:6*

Unto the upright there ariseth light in the darkness: He is gracious, and full of compassion, and righteous. *Psalm 112:4*

For the Lord giveth wisdom: out of His mouth cometh knowledge and understanding. *Proverbs 2:6*

Trust in the Lord with all thine heart; and lean not unto thine own understanding.
Proverbs 3:5

In all thy ways acknowledge Him, and He shall direct thy paths. *Proverbs 3:6*

Where no counsel is, the people fall: but in the multitude of counsellors there is safety. *Proverbs 11:14*

Without counsel purposes are disappointed: but in the multitude of counsellors they are established.
Proverbs 15:22

Every purpose is established by counsel: and with good advice make war.
Proverbs 20:18

And thine ears shall hear a word behind thee, saying, This is the way, walk ye in it, when ye turn to the right hand, and when ye turn to the left. *Isaiah 30:21*

And I will bring the blind by a way that they knew not; I will lead them in paths that they have not known: I will make darkness light before them, and crooked things straight. These things will I do unto them, and not forsake them. *Isaiah 42:16*

Thus saith the Lord, thy Redeemer, the Holy One of Israel; I am the Lord thy God which teacheth thee to profit, which leadeth thee by the way that thou shouldest go.
Isaiah 48:17

Howbeit when He, the Spirit of truth, is come, He will guide you into all truth: for He shall not speak of Himself; but whatsoever He shall hear, that shall He speak: and He will shew you things to come.
John 16:13

He shall glorify Me: for He shall receive of Mine, and shall shew it unto you.
John 16:14

If any of you lack wisdom, let him ask of God, that giveth to all men liberally, and upbraideth not; and it shall be given him.
James 1:5

72

DECISIVENESS

And if it seem evil unto you to serve the Lord, choose you this day whom ye will serve; whether the gods which your fathers served that were on the other side of the flood, or the gods of the Amorites, in whose land ye dwell: but as for me and my house, we will serve the Lord. *Joshua 24:15*

I will not be afraid of ten thousands of people, that have set themselves against me round about. *Psalm 3:6*

But as for me, I will walk in mine integrity: redeem me, and be merciful unto me. *Psalm 26:11*

Though an host should encamp against me, my heart shall not fear: though war should rise against me, in this will I be confident. *Psalm 27:3*

For in the time of trouble He shall hide

me in His pavilion: in the secret of His tabernacle shall He hide me; He shall set me up upon a rock. *Psalm 27:5*

God is our refuge and strength, a very present help in trouble. *Psalm 46:1*

Therefore will not we fear, though the earth be removed, and though the mountains be carried into the midst of the sea;
Psalm 46:2

My flesh and my heart faileth: but God is the strength of my heart, and my portion for ever. *Psalm 73:26*

See then that ye walk circumspectly, not as fools, but as wise, *Ephesians 5:15*

Walk in wisdom toward them that are without, redeeming the time.
Colossians 4:5

For the which cause I also suffer these things: nevertheless I am not ashamed: for I know whom I have believed, and am persuaded that He is able to keep that which I have committed unto Him against that day.
2 Timothy 1:12

73

DEPRESSION

Be of good courage, and He shall strengthen your heart, all ye that hope in the Lord. *Psalm 31:24*

Behold, the eye of the Lord is upon them that fear Him, upon them that hope in His mercy; *Psalm 33:18*

For in Thee, O Lord, do I hope: Thou wilt hear, O Lord my God. *Psalm 38:15*

Why art thou cast down, O my soul? and why art thou disquieted within me? hope in God: for I shall yet praise Him, Who is the health of my countenance, and my God. *Psalm 43:5*

But I will hope continually, and will yet praise Thee more and more. *Psalm 71:14*

Happy is he that hath the God of Jacob for his help, whose hope is in the Lord his God: *Psalm 146:5*

Hope deferred maketh the heart sick: but when the desire cometh, it is a tree of life. *Proverbs 13:12*

Let not thine heart envy sinners: but be thou in the fear of the Lord all the day long. *Proverbs 23:17*

For surely there is an end; and thine expectation shall not be cut off.
Proverbs 23:18

Who against hope believed in hope, that he might become the father of many nations, according to that which was spoken, So shall thy seed be. *Romans 4:18*

Now the God of hope fill you with all joy and peace in believing, that ye may abound in hope, through the power of the Holy Ghost. *Romans 15:13*

And God is able to make all grace abound toward you; that ye, always having all sufficiency in all things, may abound to every good work: *2 Corinthians 9:8*

Therefore I take pleasure in infirmities, in reproaches, in necessities, in persecutions, in distresses for Christ's sake: for when I

am weak, then am I strong.
2 Corinthians 12:10

That He would grant you, according to the riches of His glory, to be strengthened with might by His Spirit in the inner man;
Ephesians 3:16

Wherefore take unto you the whole armour of God, that ye may be able to withstand in the evil day, and having done all, to stand. *Ephesians 6:13*

Praying always with all prayer and supplication in the Spirit, and watching thereunto with all perseverance and supplication for all saints; *Ephesians 6:18*

Wherefore gird up the loins of your mind, be sober, and hope to the end for the grace that is to be brought unto you at the revelation of Jesus Christ; *1 Peter 1:13*

But the word of the Lord endureth for ever. And this is the word which by the gospel is preached unto you. *1 Peter 1:25*

74

DILIGENCE

He becometh poor that dealeth with a slack hand: but the hand of the diligent maketh rich. *Proverbs 10:4*

The hand of the diligent shall bear rule: but the slothful shall be under tribute. *Proverbs 12:24*

The slothful man roasteth not that which he took in hunting: but the substance of a diligent man is precious. *Proverbs 12:27*

The soul of the sluggard desireth, and hath nothing: but the soul of the diligent shall be made fat. *Proverbs 13:4*

The thoughts of the diligent tend only to plenteousness; but of every one that is hasty only to want. *Proverbs 21:5*

Seest thou a man diligent in his business? he shall stand before kings; he shall not stand before mean men.
Proverbs 22:29

Be thou diligent to know the state of thy flocks, and look well to thy herds.
Proverbs 27:23

Whatsoever thy hand findeth to do, do it with thy might; for there is no work, nor device, nor knowledge, nor wisdom, in the grave, whither thou goest.
Ecclesiastes 9:10

But he that knew not, and did commit things worthy of stripes, shall be beaten with few stripes. For unto whomsoever much is given, of him shall be much required: and to whom men have committed much, of him they will ask the more. *Luke 12:48*

Jesus saith unto them, My meat is to do the will of Him that sent Me, and to finish His work. *John 4:34*

I have glorified thee on the earth: I have finished the work which thou gavest me to do. *John 17:4*

Therefore, my beloved brethren, be ye stedfast, unmoveable, always abounding in the work of the Lord, forasmuch as ye know that your labour is not in vain in the Lord.
1 Corinthians 15:58

And we desire that every one of you do shew the same diligence to the full assurance of hope unto the end: *Hebrews 6:11*

That ye be not slothful, but followers of them who through faith and patience inherit the promises. *Hebrews 6:12*

75

ENCOURAGEMENT

Have not I commanded thee? Be strong and of a good courage; be not afraid, neither be thou dismayed: for the Lord thy God is with thee whithersoever thou goest.
Joshua 1:9

And he said, Hearken ye, all Judah, and ye inhabitants of Jerusalem, and thou king Jehoshaphat, Thus saith the Lord unto you, Be not afraid nor dismayed by reason of this great multitude; for the battle is not yours, but God's. *2 Chronicles 20:15*

For they all made us afraid, saying, Their hands shall be weakened from the work, that it be not done. Now therefore, O God, strengthen my hands. *Nehemiah 6:9*

In famine He shall redeem thee from death: and in war from the power of the sword. *Job 5:20*

Thou shalt be hid from the scourge of the tongue: neither shalt thou be afraid of destruction when it cometh. *Job 5:21*

Commit thy way unto the Lord; trust also in Him; and He shall bring it to pass.
Psalm 37:5

Cast thy burden upon the Lord, and He shall sustain thee: He shall never suffer the righteous to be moved. *Psalm 55:22*

Commit thy works unto the Lord, and thy thoughts shall be established.
Proverbs 16:3

The fear of man bringeth a snare: but whoso putteth his trust in the Lord shall be safe. *Proverbs 29:25*

Blessed is the man that trusteth in the Lord, and whose hope the Lord is.
Jeremiah 17:7

Be not ye therefore like unto them: for your Father knoweth what things ye have need of, before ye ask Him. *Matthew 6:8*

Behold the fowls of the air: for they sow

not, neither do they reap, nor gather into barns; yet your heavenly Father feedeth them. Are ye not much better than they?
Matthew 6:26

Jesus said unto him, If thou canst believe, all things are possible to him that believeth. *Mark 9:23*

For verily I say unto you, That whosoever shall say unto this mountain, Be thou removed, and be thou cast into the sea; and shall not doubt in his heart, but shall believe that those things which he saith shall come to pass; he shall have whatsoever he saith. *Mark 11:23*

Therefore I say unto you, What things soever ye desire, when ye pray, believe that ye receive them, and ye shall have them.
Mark 11:24

Peace I leave with you, My peace I give unto you: not as the world giveth, give I unto you. Let not your heart be troubled, neither let it be afraid. *John 14:27*

Be careful for nothing; but in every

thing by prayer and supplication with thanksgiving let your requests be made known unto God. *Philippians 4:6*

Let us therefore come boldly unto the throne of grace, that we may obtain mercy, and find grace to help in time of need.
Hebrews 4:16

Cast not away therefore your confidence, which hath great recompence of reward. *Hebrews 10:35*

76

Faith

And they that know Thy name will put their trust in Thee: for Thou, Lord, hast not forsaken them that seek Thee. *Psalm 9:10*

Trust in the Lord, and do good; so shalt thou dwell in the land, and verily thou shalt be fed.
Delight thyself also in the Lord; and He shall give thee the desires of thine heart.
Commit thy way unto the Lord; trust also in Him; and He shall bring it to pass.
Psalm 37:3-5

Thou wilt keep him in perfect peace, whose mind is stayed on Thee: because he trusteth in Thee. *Isaiah 26:3*

Blessed is the man that trusteth in the Lord, and whose hope the Lord is.
Jeremiah 17:7

And when He was come into the house,

the blind men came to Him: and Jesus saith unto them, Believe ye that I am able to do this? They said unto Him, Yea, Lord.

Then touched He their eyes, saying, According to your faith be it unto you.

Matthew 9:28,29

And Jesus said unto them, Because of your unbelief: for verily I say unto you, If ye have faith as a grain of mustard seed, ye shall say unto this mountain, Remove hence to yonder place; and it shall remove; and nothing shall be impossible unto you.

Matthew 17:20

And all things, whatsoever ye shall ask in prayer, believing, ye shall receive.

Matthew 21:22

Jesus said unto him, If thou canst believe, all things are possible to him that believeth.

Mark 9:23

And Jesus answering saith unto them, Have faith in God.

For verily I say unto you, That whosoever shall say unto this mountain, Be thou removed, and be thou cast into the sea; and shall not doubt in his heart, but shall believe that those things which he saith shall come to pass; he shall have whatsoever he saith.

Therefore I say unto you, What things soever ye desire, when ye pray, believe that ye receive them, and ye shall have them.
Mark 11:22-24

So then faith cometh by hearing, and hearing by the word of God. *Romans 10:17*

For I say, through the grace given unto me, to every man that is among you, not to think of himself more highly than he ought to think; but to think soberly, according as God hath dealt to every man the measure of faith. *Romans 12:3*

Above all, taking the shield of faith, wherewith ye shall be able to quench all the fiery darts of the wicked. *Ephesians 6:16*

Cast not away therefore your confidence, which hath great recompence of reward. *Hebrews 10:35*

Now faith is the substance of things hoped for, the evidence of things not seen.

But without faith it is impossible to

please Him; for he that cometh to God must believe that He is, and that He is a rewarder of them that diligently seek Him.
Hebrews 11:1,6

Looking unto Jesus the author and finisher of our faith; Who for the joy that was set before Him endured the cross, despising the shame, and is set down at the right hand of the throne of God. *Hebrews 12:2*

Let your conversation be without covetousness; and be content with such things as ye have: for He hath said, I will never leave thee, nor forsake thee.

So that we may boldly say, The Lord is my helper, and I will not fear what man shall do unto me. *Hebrews 13:5,6*

Behold, the hire of the labourers who have reaped down your fields, which is of you kept back by fraud, crieth: and the cries of them which have reaped are entered into the ears of the Lord of Sabaoth.

And the prayer of faith shall save the sick, and the Lord shall raise him up; and if he have committed sins, they shall be forgiven him. *James 5:4,15*

That the trial of your faith, being much more precious than of gold that perisheth, though it be tried with fire, might be found unto praise and honour and glory at the appearing of Jesus Christ:

Whom having not seen, ye love; in Whom, though now ye see Him not, yet believing, ye rejoice with joy unspeakable and full of glory:

Receiving the end of your faith, even the salvation of your souls. *1 Peter 1:7-9*

For whatsoever is born of God overcometh the world: and this is the victory that overcometh the world, even our faith.
1 John 5:4

77

Favor

But the Lord was with Joseph, and shewed him mercy, and gave him favour in the sight of the keeper of the prison.
Genesis 39:21

The Lord bless thee, and keep thee:
Numbers 6:24

The Lord make His face shine upon thee, and be gracious unto thee:
Numbers 6:25

The Lord lift up His countenance upon thee, and give thee peace. *Numbers 6:26*

Teach me, and I will hold my tongue: and cause me to understand wherein I have erred. *Job 6:24*

He shall pray unto God, and He will be favourable unto him: and He shall see his face with joy: for He will render unto man His righteousness. *Job 33:26*

The Lord hear thee in the day of trouble; the name of the God of Jacob defend thee;
Psalm 20:1

Send thee help from the sanctuary, and strengthen thee out of Zion; *Psalm 20:2*

The meek will He guide in judgment: and the meek will He teach His way.
Psalm 25:9

What man is he that feareth the Lord? him shall He teach in the way that he shall choose. *Psalm 25:12*

My times are in Thy hand: deliver me from the hand of mine enemies, and from them that persecute me. *Psalm 31:15*

Make Thy face to shine upon Thy servant: save me for Thy mercies' sake.
Psalm 31:16

Let them curse, but bless Thou: when they arise, let them be ashamed; but let Thy servant rejoice. *Psalm 109:28*

Let not mercy and truth forsake thee:

bind them about thy neck; write them upon the table of thine heart: *Proverbs 3:3*

So shalt thou find favour and good understanding in the sight of God and man.
Proverbs 3:4

For whoso findeth Me findeth life, and shall obtain favour of the Lord.
Proverbs 8:35

He that diligently seeketh good procureth favour: but he that seeketh mischief, it shall come unto him.
Proverbs 11:27

When a man's ways please the Lord, He maketh even his enemies to be at peace with him. *Proverbs 16:7*

For he that in these things serveth Christ is acceptable to God, and approved of men. *Romans 14:18*

Let us therefore come boldly unto the throne of grace, that we may obtain mercy, and find grace to help in time of need.
Hebrews 4:16

78

FORGIVENESS

The discretion of a man deferreth his anger; and it is his glory to pass over a transgression. *Proverbs 19:11*

Rejoice not when thine enemy falleth, and let not thine heart be glad when he stumbleth: *Proverbs 24:17*

Say not, I will do so to him as he hath done to me: I will render to the man according to his work. *Proverbs 24:29*

If thine enemy be hungry, give him bread to eat; and if he be thirsty, give him water to drink: *Proverbs 25:21*

Blessed are the merciful: for they shall obtain mercy. *Matthew 5:7*

But I say unto you, That ye resist not evil: but whosoever shall smite thee on thy

right cheek, turn to him the other also.
Matthew 5:39

But I say unto you, Love your enemies, bless them that curse you, do good to them that hate you, and pray for them which despitefully use you, and persecute you;
Matthew 5:44

And forgive us our debts, as we forgive our debtors.
Matthew 6:12

For if ye forgive men their trespasses, your heavenly Father will also forgive you:
Matthew 6:14

But if ye forgive not men their trespasses, neither will your Father forgive your trespasses.
Matthew 6:15

And when ye stand praying, forgive, if ye have ought against any: that your Father also which is in heaven may forgive you your trespasses.
Mark 11:25

Take heed to yourselves: If thy brother trespass against thee, rebuke him; and if he repent, forgive him.
Luke 17:3

And if he trespass against thee seven times in a day, and seven times in a day turn again to thee, saying, I repent; thou shalt forgive him. *Luke 17:4*

Bless them which persecute you: bless, and curse not. *Romans 12:14*

Be not overcome of evil, but overcome evil with good. *Romans 12:21*

And be ye kind one to another, tenderhearted, forgiving one another, even as God for Christ's sake hath forgiven you. *Ephesians 4:32*

Forbearing one another, and forgiving one another, if any man have a quarrel against any: even as Christ forgave you, so also do ye. *Colossians 3:13*

Not rendering evil for evil, or railing for railing: but contrariwise blessing; knowing that ye are thereunto called, that ye should inherit a blessing. *1 Peter 3:9*

79

GOAL-SETTING

I wisdom dwell with prudence, and find out knowledge of witty inventions.
Proverbs 8:12

A man shall be commended according to his wisdom: but he that is of a perverse heart shall be despised. *Proverbs 12:8*

Every prudent man dealeth with knowledge: but a fool layeth open his folly.
Proverbs 13:16

The simple believeth every word: but the prudent man looketh well to his going.
Proverbs 14:15

A wise man feareth, and departeth from evil: but the fool rageth, and is confident.
Proverbs 14:16

Without counsel purposes are

disappointed: but in the multitude of counsellors they are established.
Proverbs 15:22

He that handleth a matter wisely shall find good: and whoso trusteth in the Lord, happy is he. *Proverbs 16:20*

The heart of the prudent getteth knowledge; and the ear of the wise seeketh knowledge. *Proverbs 18:15*

Counsel in the heart of man is like deep water; but a man of understanding will draw it out. *Proverbs 20:5*

Every purpose is established by counsel: and with good advice make war.
Proverbs 20:18

The thoughts of the diligent tend only to plenteousness; but of every one that is hasty only to want. *Proverbs 21:5*

For by wise counsel thou shalt make thy war: and in the multitude of counsellors there is safety. *Proverbs 24:6*

Go not forth hastily to strive, lest thou know not what to do in the end thereof, when thy neighbour hath put thee to shame.
Proverbs 25:8

If the iron be blunt, and he do not whet the edge, then must he put to more strength: but wisdom is profitable to direct.
Ecclesiastes 10:10

For which of you, intending to build a tower, sitteth not down first, and counteth the cost, whether he have sufficient to finish it?
Luke 14:28

Lest haply, after he hath laid the foundation, and is not able to finish it, all that behold it begin to mock him,
Luke 14:29

Saying, This man began to build, and was not able to finish.
Luke 14:30

Or what king, going to make war against another king, sitteth not down first, and consulteth whether he be able with ten thousand to meet him that cometh against him with twenty thousand?
Luke 14:31

80

HEALING

And said, If thou wilt diligently hearken to the voice of the Lord thy God, and wilt do that which is right in His sight, and wilt give ear to His commandments, and keep all His statutes, I will put none of these diseases upon thee, which I have brought upon the Egyptians: for I am the Lord that healeth thee. *Exodus 15:26*

And ye shall serve the Lord your God, and He shall bless thy bread, and thy water; and I will take sickness away from the midst of thee.
There shall nothing cast their young, nor be barren, in thy land: the number of thy days I will fulfil. *Exodus 23:25,26*

For the eyes of the Lord run to and fro throughout the whole earth, to shew Himself strong in the behalf of them whose heart is perfect toward Him. Herein thou hast done foolishly: therefore from henceforth thou shalt have wars. *2 Chronicles 16:9*

There shall no evil befall thee, neither shall any plague come nigh thy dwelling.
Psalm 91:10

With long life will I satisfy him, and shew him My salvation. *Psalm 91:16*

Bless the Lord, O my soul, and forget not all His benefits:
Who forgiveth all thine iniquities; Who healeth all thy diseases; *Psalm 103:2,3*

He sent His word, and healed them, and delivered them from their destructions.
Psalm 107:20

Surely He hath borne our griefs, and carried our sorrows: yet we did esteem Him stricken, smitten of God, and afflicted.
But He was wounded for our transgressions, He was bruised for our iniquities: the chastisement of our peace was upon Him; and with His stripes we are healed. *Isaiah 53:4,5*

So shall My word be that goeth forth out of My mouth: it shall not return unto Me void, but it shall accomplish that which I please, and it shall prosper in the thing whereto I sent it. *Isaiah 55:11*

And, behold, there came a leper and worshipped Him saying, Lord, if Thou wilt, Thou canst make me clean.

And Jesus put forth His hand, and touched Him, saying, I will; be thou clean. And immediately his leprosy was cleansed.
Matthew 8:2,3

When the even was come, they brought unto Him many that were possessed with devils: and He cast out the spirits with His word, and healed all that were sick:

That it might be fulfilled which was spoken by Esaias the prophet, saying, Himself took our infirmities, and bare our sicknesses. *Matthew 8:16,17*

For verily I say unto you, That whosoever shall say unto this mountain, Be thou removed, and be thou cast into the sea; and shall not doubt in his heart, but shall believe that those things which he saith shall come to pass; he shall have whatsoever he saith.

Therefore I say unto you, What things soever ye desire, when ye pray, believe that ye receive them, and ye shall have them.
Mark 11:23,24

Jesus heard that they had cast him out;

and when He had found him, He said unto him, Dost thou believe on the Son of God?
John 9:35

The thief cometh not, but for to steal, and to kill, and to destroy: I am come that they might have life, and that they might have it more abundantly. *John 10:10*

Verily, verily, I say unto you, He that believeth on Me, the works that I do shall he do also; and greater works than these shall he do; because I go unto My Father.
John 14:12

How God anointed Jesus of Nazareth with the Holy Ghost and with power: Who went about doing good, and healing all that were oppressed of the devil; for God was with Him. *Acts 10:38*

Christ hath redeemed us from the curse of the law, being made a curse for us: for it is written, Cursed is every one that hangeth on a tree. *Galatians 3:13*

Jesus Christ the same yesterday, and to day, and for ever. *Hebrews 13:8*

Every good gift and every perfect gift is from above, and cometh down from the Father of lights, with Whom is no variableness, neither shadow of turning.
James 1:17

Is any sick among you? let him call for the elders of the church; and let them pray over him, anointing him with oil in the name of the Lord:
And the prayer of faith shall save the sick, and the Lord shall raise him up; and if he have committed sins, they shall be forgiven him. *James 5:14,15*

Who His own self bare our sins in His own body on the tree, that we, being dead to sins, should live unto righteousness: by Whose stripes ye were healed. *1 Peter 2:24*

Ye are of God, little children, and have overcome them: because greater is He that is in you, than he that is in the world.
1 John 4:4

Beloved, I wish above all things that thou mayest prosper and be in health, even as thy soul prospereth. *3 John 2*

81

HONESTY

Ye shall do no unrighteousness in judgment, in meteyard, in weight, or in measure. *Leviticus 19:35*

That which is altogether just shalt thou follow, that thou mayest live, and inherit the land which the Lord thy God giveth thee.
Deuteronomy 16:20

Thou shalt not have in thy bag divers weights, a great and a small.
Deuteronomy 25:13

But thou shalt have a perfect and just weight, a perfect and just measure shalt thou have: that thy days may be lengthened in the land which the Lord thy God giveth thee.
Deuteronomy 25:15

For all that do such things, and all that do unrighteously, are an abomination unto the Lord thy God. *Deuteronomy 25:16*

He that putteth not out his money to usury, nor taketh reward against the innocent. He that doeth these things shall never be moved. *Psalm 15:5*

A false balance is abomination to the Lord: but a just weight is His delight.
Proverbs 11:1

Lying lips are abomination to the Lord: but they that deal truly are His delight.
Proverbs 12:22

He that walketh righteously, and speaketh uprightly; he that despiseth the gain of oppressions, that shaketh his hands from holding of bribes, that stoppeth his ears from hearing of blood, and shutteth his eyes from seeing evil; *Isaiah 33:15*

And as ye would that men should do to you, do ye also to them likewise. *Luke 6:31*

And herein do I exercise myself, to have always a conscience void of offence toward God, and toward men. *Acts 24:16*

But have renounced the hidden things of dishonesty, not walking in craftiness, nor handling the word of God deceitfully; but by manifestation of the truth commending ourselves to every man's conscience in the sight of God. *2 Corinthians 4:2*

Receive us; we have wronged no man, we have corrupted no man, we have defrauded no man. *2 Corinthians 7:2*

Providing for honest things, not only in the sight of the Lord, but also in the sight of men. *2 Corinthians 8:21*

Finally, brethren, whatsoever things are true, whatsoever things are honest, whatsoever things are just, whatsoever things are pure, whatsoever things are lovely, whatsoever things are of good report; if there be any virtue, and if there be any praise, think on these things. *Philippians 4:8*

That ye may walk honestly toward them that are without, and that ye may have lack of nothing. *1 Thessalonians 4:12*

Having your conversation honest among the Gentiles: that, whereas they speak against you as evildoers, they may by your good works, which they shall behold, glorify God in the day of visitation.
1 Peter 2:12

When You Want Something
You Have Never Had,
You Have Got To Do Something
You Have Never Done.

-MIKE MURDOCK

Copyright © 2001 by Mike Murdock • Wisdom International
The Wisdom Center • P.O. Box 99 • Denton, TX 76202

82

IDEAS

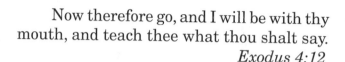

Now therefore go, and I will be with thy mouth, and teach thee what thou shalt say.
Exodus 4:12

But there is a spirit in man: and the inspiration of the Almighty giveth them understanding. *Job 32:8*

Then He openeth the ears of men, and sealeth their instruction, *Job 33:16*

I will bless the Lord, Who hath given me counsel: my reins also instruct me in the night seasons. *Psalm 16:7*

I will instruct thee and teach thee in the way which thou shalt go: I will guide thee with Mine eye. *Psalm 32:8*

For with Thee is the fountain of life: in Thy light shall we see light. *Psalm 36:9*

Many, O Lord my God, are Thy wonderful works which Thou hast done, and Thy thoughts which are to us-ward: they cannot be reckoned up in order unto Thee: if I would declare and speak of them, they are more than can be numbered.
Psalm 40:5

The Lord will perfect that which concerneth me: Thy mercy, O Lord, endureth for ever: forsake not the works of Thine own hands. *Psalm 138:8*

I love them that love Me; and those that seek Me early shall find Me. *Proverbs 8:17*

The thoughts of the righteous are right: but the counsels of the wicked are deceit.
Proverbs 12:5

So shall the knowledge of wisdom be unto thy soul: when thou hast found it, then there shall be a reward, and thy expectation shall not be cut off. *Proverbs 24:14*

Behold, the former things are come to pass, and new things do I declare: before they spring forth I tell you of them.
Isaiah 42:9

Behold, I will do a new thing; now it shall spring forth; shall ye not know it? I will even make a way in the wilderness, and rivers in the desert. *Isaiah 43:19*

Thou hast heard, see all this; and will not ye declare it? I have shewed thee new things from this time, even hidden things, and thou didst not know them. *Isaiah 48:6*

They are created now, and not from the beginning; even before the day when thou heardest them not; lest thou shouldest say, Behold, I knew them. *Isaiah 48:7*

For I know the thoughts that I think toward you, saith the Lord, thoughts of peace, and not of evil, to give you an expected end. *Jeremiah 29:11*

83

INTEGRITY

The wicked borroweth, and payeth not again: but the righteous sheweth mercy, and giveth. *Psalm 37:21*

And as for me, Thou upholdest me in mine integrity, and settest me before Thy face for ever. *Psalm 41:12*

A good man sheweth favour, and lendeth: he will guide his affairs with discretion. *Psalm 112:5*

A false balance is abomination to the Lord: but a just weight is his delight.
Proverbs 11:1

The integrity of the upright shall guide them: but the perverseness of transgressors shall destroy them. *Proverbs 11:3*

Better is a little with righteousness than great revenues without right.
Proverbs 16:8

The just man walketh in his integrity: his children are blessed after him.

Proverbs 20:7

The getting of treasures by a lying tongue is a vanity tossed to and fro of them that seek death. *Proverbs 21:6*

He that oppresseth the poor to increase his riches, and he that giveth to the rich, shall surely come to want. *Proverbs 22:16*

Woe unto him that buildeth his house by unrighteousness, and his chambers by wrong; that useth his neighbour's service without wages, and giveth him not for his work; *Jeremiah 22:13*

Give to him that asketh thee, and from him that would borrow of thee turn not thou away. *Matthew 5:42*

And He said unto them, Exact no more than that which is appointed you.

Luke 3:13

And if ye have not been faithful in that which is another man's, who shall give you that which is your own? *Luke 16:12*

And Zacchaeus stood, and said unto the Lord; Behold, Lord, the half of my goods I give to the poor; and if I have taken any thing from any man by false accusation, I restore him fourfold. *Luke 19:8*

Receive us; we have wronged no man, we have corrupted no man, we have defrauded no man. *2 Corinthians 7:2*

84

LEADERSHIP

Ye shall do no unrighteousness in judgment: thou shalt not respect the person of the poor, nor honour the person of the mighty: but in righteousness shalt thou judge thy neighbour.
Leviticus 19:15

The God of Israel said, the Rock of Israel spake to me, He that ruleth over men must be just, ruling in the fear of God.
2 Samuel 23:3

Be wise now therefore, O ye kings; be instructed, ye judges of the earth.
Psalm 2:10

The meek will He guide in judgment: and the meek will He teach His way.
Psalm 25:9

Thou shalt guide me with Thy counsel, and afterward receive me to glory.
Psalm 73:24

These things also belong to the wise. It is not good to have respect of persons in judgment. *Proverbs 24:23*

Thus speaketh the Lord of hosts, saying, Execute true judgment, and shew mercy and compassions every man to his brother:
Zechariah 7:9

And oppress not the widow, nor the fatherless, the stranger, nor the poor; and let none of you imagine evil against his brother in your heart. *Zechariah 7:10*

For with what judgment ye judge, ye shall be judged: and with what measure ye mete, it shall be measured to you again.
Matthew 7:2

For as many as are led by the Spirit of God, they are the sons of God.
Romans 8:14

For kings, and for all that are in authority; that we may lead a quiet and peaceable life in all godliness and honesty.
1 Timothy 2:2

The Quality Of A Nation
    Is Revealed By The Quality
Of The Leader
    God Permits To Govern It.

—MIKE MURDOCK

Copyright © 2001 by Mike Murdock • Wisdom International
The Wisdom Center • P.O. Box 99 • Denton, TX 76202

85

LONELINESS

The eternal God is thy refuge, and underneath are the everlasting arms: and He shall thrust out the enemy from before thee; and shall say, Destroy them.
Deuteronomy 33:27

And they that know Thy name will put their trust in Thee: for Thou, Lord, hast not forsaken them that seek Thee. *Psalm 9:10*

Yea, though I walk through the valley of the shadow of death, I will fear no evil: for Thou art with me; Thy rod and Thy staff they comfort me. *Psalm 23:4*

I have been young, and now am old; yet have I not seen the righteous forsaken, nor His seed begging bread. *Psalm 37:25*

For the Lord loveth judgment, and forsaketh not His saints; they are preserved for ever: but the seed of the wicked shall be cut off. *Psalm 37:28*

Save me, O God; for the waters are come in unto my soul. *Psalm 69:1*

I sink in deep mire, where there is no standing: I am come into deep waters, where the floods overflow me. *Psalm 69:2*

I am weary of my crying: my throat is dried: mine eyes fail while I wait for my God. *Psalm 69:3*

He healeth the broken in heart, and bindeth up their wounds. *Psalm 147:3*

For Thou hast been a strength to the poor, a strength to the needy in his distress, a refuge from the storm, a shadow from the heat, when the blast of the terrible ones is as a storm against the wall. *Isaiah 25:4*

He giveth power to the faint; and to them that have no might He increaseth strength. *Isaiah 40:29*

Fear thou not; for I am with thee: be not dismayed; for I am thy God: I will strengthen thee; yea, I will help thee; yea, I will uphold thee with the right hand of My righteousness. *Isaiah 41:10*

But the very hairs of your head are all numbered. *Matthew 10:30*

And I will pray the Father, and he shall give you another Comforter, that He may abide with you for ever; *John 14:16*

Even the Spirit of truth; Whom the world cannot receive, because it seeth Him not, neither knoweth Him: but ye know Him; for He dwelleth with you, and shall be in you.
John 14:17

I will not leave you comfortless: I will come to you. *John 14:18*

At my first answer no man stood with me, but all men forsook me: I pray God that it may not be laid to their charge.
2 Timothy 4:16

Notwithstanding the Lord stood with me, and strengthened me; that by me the preaching might be fully known, and that

all the Gentiles might hear: and I was delivered out of the mouth of the lion.
2 Timothy 4:17

And the Lord shall deliver me from every evil work, and will preserve me unto His heavenly kingdom: to Whom be glory for ever and ever. Amen. *2 Timothy 4:18*

Let us therefore come boldly unto the throne of grace, that we may obtain mercy, and find grace to help in time of need.
Hebrews 4:16

Let your conversation be without covetousness; and be content with such things as ye have: for He hath said, I will never leave thee, nor forsake thee.
Hebrews 13:5

86

LOVE

And thou shalt love the Lord thy God with all thine heart, and with all thy soul, and with all thy might.   *Deuteronomy 6:5*

And now, Israel, what doth the Lord thy God require of thee, but to fear the Lord thy God, to walk in all His ways, and to love Him, and to serve the Lord thy God with all thy heart and will all thy soul,
Deuteronomy 10:12

But take diligent heed to do the commandment and the law, which Moses the servant of the Lord charged you, to love the Lord your God, and to walk in all His ways, and to keep His commandments, and to cleave unto Him, and to serve Him with all your heart and with all your soul.
Joshua 22:5

I love the Lord, because He hath heard my voice and my supplications.   *Psalm 116:1*

Hatred stirreth up strifes: but love covereth all sins. *Proverbs 10:12*

He that covereth a transgression seeketh love; but he that repeateth a matter separateth very friends. *Proverbs 17:9*

A friend loveth at all times, and a brother is born for adversity. *Proverbs 17:17*

Set me as a seal upon thine heart, as a seal upon thine arm: for love is strong as death; jealousy is cruel as the grave: the coals thereof are coals of fire, which hath a most vehement flame.
Many waters cannot quench love, neither can the floods drown it: if a man would give all the substance of his house for love, it would utterly be contemned.
Song of Solomon 8:6,7

Honor thy father and thy mother: and, Thou shalt love thy neighbour as thyself.
Matthew 19:19

And Jesus answered and said unto them, I will also ask of you one question, and answer Me, and I will tell you by what authority I do these things.

The baptism of John, was it from heaven, or of men? answer Me.

And they reasoned with themselves, saying, If we shall say, From heaven; He will say, Why then did ye not believe him?

But if we shall say, Of men; they feared the people: for all men counted John, that he was a prophet indeed.

And they answered and said unto Jesus, We cannot tell. And Jesus answering saith unto them, Neither do I tell you by what authority I do these things. *Mark 11:29-33*

A new commandment I give unto you, That ye love one another; as I have loved you, that ye also love one another.

By this shall all men know that ye are My disciples, if ye have love one to another.
John 13:34,35

And hope maketh not ashamed; because the love of God is shed abroad in our hearts by the Holy Ghost which is given unto us.
Romans 5:5

Now as touching things offered unto idols, we know that we all have knowledge. Knowledge puffeth up, but charity edifieth.
1 Corinthians 8:1

And this I pray, that your love may abound yet more and more in knowledge and in all judgment;

That ye may approve things that are excellent; that ye may be sincere and without offence till the day of Christ;

Being filled with the fruits of righteousness, which are by Jesus Christ, unto the glory and praise of God.

Philippians 1:9-11

And the Lord make you to increase and abound in love one toward another, and toward all men, even as we do toward you:

To the end He may stablish your hearts unblamable in holiness before God, even our Father, at the coming of our Lord Jesus Christ with all His saints.

1 Thessalonians 3:12,13

But as touching brotherly love ye need not that I write unto you: for ye yourselves are taught of God to love one another.

And indeed ye do it toward all the brethren which are in all Macedonia: but we beseech you, brethren, that ye increase more and more; *1 Thessalonians 4:9,10*

And the Lord direct your hearts into the

love of God, and into the patient waiting for Christ. *2 Thessalonians 3:5*

Now the end of the commandment is charity out of a pure heart, and of a good conscience, and of faith unfeigned:
1 Timothy 1:5

Desiring to be teachers of the law; understanding neither what they say, nor whereof they affirm. *1 Timothy 1:7*

And above all things have fervent charity among yourselves: for charity shall cover the multitude of sins. *1 Peter 4:8*

He that loveth his brother abideth in the light, and there is none occasion of stumbling in him. *1 John 2:10*

Herein is love, not that we loved God, but that He loved us, and sent His Son to be the propitiation for our sins.
Beloved, if God so loved us, we ought also to love one another.
No man hath seen God at any time. If we love one another, God dwelleth in us, and His love is perfected in us. *1 John 4:10-12*

And we have known and believed the love that God hath to us. God is love; and he that dwelleth in love dwelleth in God, and God in him.

Herein is our love made perfect, that we may have boldness in the day of judgment: because as He is, so are we in this world.

There is no fear in love; but perfect love casteth out fear: because fear hath torment. He that feareth is not made perfect in love.
1 John 4:16-18

87

LOYALTY

O love the Lord, all ye His saints: for the Lord preserveth the faithful, and plentifully rewardeth the proud doer.
Psalm 31:23

A faithful man shall abound with blessings: but he that maketh haste to be rich shall not be innocent. *Proverbs 28:20*

Therefore turn thou to thy God: keep mercy and judgment, and wait on thy God continually. *Hosea 12:6*

Who then is a faithful and wise servant, whom his lord hath made ruler over his household, to give them meat in due season?
Matthew 24:45

Blessed is that servant, whom his lord when he cometh shall find so doing.
Matthew 24:46

His lord said unto him, Well done, thou good and faithful servant: thou hast been faithful over a few things, I will make thee ruler over many things: enter thou into the joy of thy lord. *Matthew 25:21*

He that is faithful in that which is least is faithful also in much: and he that is unjust in the least is unjust also in much.
Luke 16:10

If therefore ye have not been faithful in the unrighteous mammon, who will commit to your trust the true riches? *Luke 16:11*

And if ye have not been faithful in that which is another man's, who shall give you that which is your own? *Luke 16:12*

Moreover it is required in stewards, that a man be found faithful.
1 Corinthians 4:2

Therefore, my beloved brethren, be ye stedfast, unmoveable, always abounding in the work of the Lord, forasmuch as ye know that your labour is not in vain in the Lord.
1 Corinthians 15:58

Watch ye, stand fast in the faith, quit you like men, be strong.
1 Corinthians 16:13

Therefore, my brethren dearly beloved and longed for, my joy and crown, so stand fast in the Lord, my dearly beloved.
Philippians 4:1

For consider Him that endured such contradiction of sinners against Himself, lest ye be wearied and faint in your minds.
Hebrews 12:3

88

MOTIVATION

There shall no man be able to stand before you: for the Lord your God shall lay the fear of you and the dread of you upon all the land that ye shall tread upon, as He hath said unto you. *Deuteronomy 11:25*

The Lord shall cause thine enemies that rise up against thee to be smitten before thy face: they shall come out against thee one way, and flee before thee seven ways.
Deuteronomy 28:7

For the Lord hath driven out from before you great nations and strong: but as for you, no man hath been able to stand before you unto this day. *Joshua 23:9*

He that gathereth in summer is a wise son: but he that sleepeth in harvest is a son that causeth shame. *Proverbs 10:5*

The hand of the diligent shall bear rule: but the slothful shall be under tribute.
Proverbs 12:24

The slothful man roasteth not that which he took in hunting: but the substance of a diligent man is precious.
Proverbs 12:27

The way of the slothful man is as an hedge of thorns: but the way of the righteous is made plain. *Proverbs 15:19*

He also that is slothful in his work is brother to him that is a great waster.
Proverbs 18:9

Slothfulness casteth into a deep sleep; and an idle soul shall suffer hunger.
Proverbs 19:15

A slothful man hideth his hand in his bosom, and will not so much as bring it to his mouth again. *Proverbs 19:24*

The desire of the slothful killeth him; for his hands refuse to labour.
Proverbs 21:25

The slothful man saith, There is a lion without, I shall be slain in the streets.
Proverbs 22:13

Then I saw, and considered it well: I looked upon it, and received instruction.
Proverbs 24:32

As the door turneth upon his hinges, so doth the slothful upon his bed.
Proverbs 26:14

By much slothfulness the building decayeth; and through idleness of the hands the house droppeth through.
Ecclesiastes 10:18

No weapon that is formed against thee shall prosper; and every tongue that shall rise against thee in judgment thou shalt condemn. This is the heritage of the servants of the Lord, and their righteousness is of Me, saith the Lord.
Isaiah 54:17

Ask, and it shall be given you; seek, and ye shall find; knock, and it shall be opened unto you:
Matthew 7:7

For every one that asketh receiveth; and he that seeketh findeth; and to him that knocketh it shall be opened.   *Matthew 7:8*

For the weapons of our warfare are not carnal, but mighty through God to the pulling down of strong holds;
2 Corinthians 10:4

Walk in wisdom toward them that are without, redeeming the time.
Colossians 4:5

Let him eschew evil, and do good; let him seek peace, and ensue it.   *1 Peter 3:11*

For our eyes of the Lord are over the righteous, and His ears are open unto their prayers: but the face of the Lord is against them that do evil.   *1 Peter 3:12*

89

NEGOTIATION

Be strong and of a good courage, fear not, nor be afraid of them: for the Lord thy God, He it is that doth go with thee; He will not fail thee, nor forsake thee.
Deuteronomy 31:6

Have not I commanded thee? Be strong and of a good courage; be not afraid, neither be thou dismayed: for the Lord thy God is with thee whithersoever thou goest.
Joshua 1:9

Wait on the Lord: be of good courage, and He shall strengthen thine heart: wait, I say, on the Lord. *Psalm 27:14*

He that is slow to wrath is of great understanding: but he that is hasty of spirit exalteth folly. *Proverbs 14:29*

A wholesome tongue is a tree of life: but perverseness therein is a breach in the spirit.
Proverbs 15:4

Better it is to be of an humble spirit with the lowly, than to divide the spoil with the proud. *Proverbs 16:19*

He that handleth a matter wisely shall find good: and whoso trusteth in the Lord, happy is he. *Proverbs 16:20*

The wise in heart shall be called prudent: and the sweetness of the lips increaseth learning. *Proverbs 16:21*

The beginning of strife is as when one letteth out water: therefore leave off contention, before it be meddled with.
Proverbs 17:14

He that hath knowledge spareth his words: and a man of understanding is of an excellent spirit. *Proverbs 17:27*

He that goeth about as a talebearer revealeth secrets: therefore meddle not with him that flattereth with his lips.
Proverbs 20:19

My son, fear thou the Lord and the king: and meddle not with them that are given to change: *Proverbs 24:21*

Better is the end of a thing than the beginning thereof: and the patient in spirit is better than the proud in spirit.
Ecclesiastes 7:8

And the spirit of the Lord shall rest upon him, the spirit of wisdom and understanding, the spirit of counsel and might, the spirit of knowledge and of the fear of the Lord;
Isaiah 11:2

Blessed are the peacemakers: for they shall be called the children of God.
Matthew 5:9

And they were not able to resist the wisdom and the spirit by which He spake.
Acts 6:10

Not slothful in business; fervent in spirit; serving the Lord;
Romans 12:11

If it be possible, as much as lieth in you, live peaceably with all men.
Romans 12:18

For God hath not given us the spirit of fear; but of power, and of love, and of a sound mind.
2 Timothy 1:7

If any of you lack wisdom, let him ask of God, that giveth to all men liberally, and upbraideth not; and it shall be given him.
James 1:5

But the wisdom that is from above is first pure, then peaceable, gentle, and easy to be entreated, full of mercy and good fruits, without partiality, and without hypocrisy.
James 3:17

90

OBEDIENCE

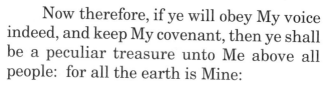

Now therefore, if ye will obey My voice indeed, and keep My covenant, then ye shall be a peculiar treasure unto Me above all people: for all the earth is Mine:
Exodus 19:5

But if thou shalt indeed obey His voice, and do all that I speak; then I will be an enemy unto thine enemies, and an adversary unto thine adversaries.
For Mine Angel shall go before thee,
Exodus 23:22,23

And it shall come to pass, if ye shall hearken diligently unto My commandments which I command you this day, to love the Lord your God, and to serve Him with all your heart and with all your soul,
That I will give you the rain of your land in his due season, the first rain and the latter rain, that thou mayest gather in thy corn, and thy wine, and thine oil.
Deuteronomy 11:13,14

Blessed is the man that walketh not in the counsel of the ungodly, nor standeth in the way of sinners, nor sitteth in the seat of the scornful.

But his delight is in the law of the Lord; and in His law doth he meditate day and night. *Psalm 1:1,2*

All the paths of the Lord are mercy and truth unto such as keep His covenant and His testimonies. *Psalm 25:10*

The fear of the Lord is the beginning of wisdom: a good understanding have all they that do His commandments: His praise endureth for ever. *Psalm 111:10*

Blessed are they that keep His testimonies, and that seek Him with the whole heart.

Thou hast commanded us to keep thy precepts diligently. *Psalm 119:2,4*

Keep My commandments, and live; and My law as the apple of thine eye.
Proverbs 7:2

He that keepeth the commandment keepeth his own soul; but he that despiseth

His ways shall die. *Proverbs 19:16*

If ye be willing and obedient, ye shall eat the good of the land: *Isaiah 1:19*

Whosoever therefore shall break one of these least commandments, and shall teach men so, he shall be called the least in the kingdom of heaven: but whosoever shall do and teach them, the same shall be called great in the kingdom of heaven.
Matthew 5:19

For whosoever shall do the will of My Father which is in heaven, the same is My brother, and sister, and mother.
Matthew 12:50

His lord said unto him, Well done, thou good and faithful servant: thou hast been faithful over a few things, I will make thee ruler over many things: enter thou into the joy of thy lord. *Matthew 25:21*

He that is faithful in that which is least is faithful also in much: and he that is unjust in the least is unjust also in much.
If therefore ye have not been faithful in the unrighteous mammon, who will commit

to your trust the true riches?

And if ye have not been faithful in that which is another man's, who shall give you that which is your own? *Luke 16:10-12*

If ye love Me, keep My commandments.

Jesus answered and said unto him, If a man love Me, he will keep My words: and My Father will love him, and We will come unto him, and make Our abode with him.
John 14:15,23

If ye keep My commandments, ye shall abide in My love; even as I have kept My Father's commandments, and abide in His love.

Ye are My friends, if ye do whatsoever I command you. *John 15:10,14*

Then Peter and the other apostles answered and said, We ought to obey God rather than men. *Acts 5:29*

Though He were a Son, yet learned He obedience by the things which He suffered;

And being made perfect, He became the author of eternal salvation unto all them that obey Him; *Hebrews 5:8,9*

Submit yourselves therefore to God. Resist the devil, and he will flee from you.
James 4:7

And whatsoever we ask, we receive of Him, because we keep His commandments, and do those things that are pleasing in His sight.

And he that keepeth His commandments dwelleth in Him, and He in him. And hereby we know that He abideth in us, by the Spirit which He hath given us.
1 John 3:22,24

~ 91 ~

PATIENCE

Rest in the Lord, and wait patiently for Him: fret not thyself because of him who prospereth in his way, because of the man who bringeth wicked devices to pass.
Psalm 37:7

Better is the end of a thing than the beginning thereof: and the patient in spirit is better than the proud in spirit.
Ecclesiastes 7:8

It is good that a man should both hope and quietly wait for the salvation of the Lord.
Lamentations 3:26

But that on the good ground are they, which in an honest and good heart, having heard the word, keep it, and bring forth fruit with patience. *Luke 8:15*

In your patience possess ye your souls.
Luke 21:19

And not only so, but we glory in tribulations also: knowing that tribulation worketh patience; *Romans 5:3*

And patience, experience; and experience, hope: *Romans 5:4*

Rejoicing in hope; patient in tribulation; continuing instant in prayer; *Romans 12:12*

But in all things approving ourselves as the ministers of God, in much patience, in afflictions, in necessities, in distresses,
2 Corinthians 6:4

In stripes, in imprisonments, in tumults, in labours, in watchings, in fastings;
2 Corinthians 6:5

By pureness, by knowledge, by longsuffering, by kindness, by the Holy Ghost, by love unfeigned, *2 Corinthians 6:6*

That ye might walk worthy of the Lord unto all pleasing, being fruitful in every good work, and increasing in the knowledge of God; *Colossians 1:10*

Strengthened with all might, according to His glorious power, unto all patience and

longsuffering with joyfulness;
Colossians 1:11

But thou, O man of God, flee these things; and follow after righteousness, godliness, faith, love, patience, meekness.
1 Timothy 6:11

And so, after he had patiently endured, he obtained the promise. *Hebrews 6:15*

For ye have need of patience, that, after ye have done the will of God, ye might receive the promise. *Hebrews 10:36*

Wherefore seeing we also are compassed about with so great a cloud of witnesses, let us lay aside every weight, and the sin which doth so easily beset us, and let us run with patience the race that is set before us, *Hebrews 12:1*

Knowing this, that the trying of your faith worketh patience. *James 1:3*

But let patience have her perfect work, that ye may be perfect and entire, wanting nothing. *James 1:4*

92

PEACE

I will both lay me down in peace, and sleep: for thou, Lord, only makest me dwell in safety. *Psalm 4:8*

His soul shall dwell at ease; and his seed shall inherit the earth. *Psalm 25:13*

The Lord will give strength unto His people; the Lord will bless His people with peace. *Psalm 29:11*

But the meek shall inherit the earth; and shall delight themselves in the abundance of peace. *Psalm 37:11*

Mark the perfect man, and behold the upright: for the end of that man is peace. *Psalm 37:37*

I will hear what God the Lord will speak: for He will speak peace unto His people, and to His saints: but let them not turn again to folly. *Psalm 85:8*

Great peace have they which love Thy law: and nothing shall offend them.
Psalm 119:165

Thou wilt keep him in perfect peace, whose mind is stayed on Thee: because he trusteth in Thee. *Isaiah 26:3*

Peace I leave with you, My peace I give unto you: not as the world giveth, give I unto you. Let not your heart be troubled, neither let it be afraid. *John 14:27*

These things I have spoken unto you, that in Me ye might have peace. In the world ye shall have tribulation: but be of good cheer; I have overcome the world.
John 16:33

For to be carnally minded is death; but to be spiritually minded is life and peace.
Romans 8:6

For the kingdom of God is not meat and drink; but righteousness, and peace, and joy in the Holy Ghost. *Romans 14:17*

Grace be to you and peace from God the Father, and from our Lord Jesus Christ,
Galatians 1:3

But the fruit of the Spirit is love, joy, peace, longsuffering, gentleness, goodness, faith, *Galatians 5:22*

For He is our peace, Who hath made both one, and hath broken down the middle wall of partition between us; *Ephesians 2:14*

And the peace of God, which passeth all understanding, shall keep your hearts and minds through Christ Jesus.
Philippians 4:7

Those things, which ye have both learned, and received, and heard, and seen in Me, do: and the God of peace shall be with you. *Philippians 4:9*

And let the peace of God rule in your hearts, to the which also ye are called in one body; and be ye thankful. *Colossians 3:15*

Now the Lord of peace Himself give you peace always by all means. The Lord be with you all. *2 Thessalonians 3:16*

But the wisdom that is from above is first pure, then peaceable, gentle, and easy to be intreated, full of mercy and good fruits, without partiality, and without hypocrisy.
James 3:17

93

PRAISE

I will call on the Lord, Who is worthy to be praised: so shall I be saved from mine enemies. *2 Samuel 22:4*

Give unto the Lord the glory due unto His name: bring an offering, and come before Him: worship the Lord in the beauty of holiness. *1 Chronicles 16:29*

And they sang together by course in praising and giving thanks unto the Lord; because He is good, for His mercy endureth for ever toward Israel. And all the people shouted with a great shout, when they praised the Lord, because the foundation of the house of the Lord was laid. *Ezra 3:11*

But as for me, I will come into Thy house in the multitude of thy mercy: and in Thy fear will I worship toward thy holy temple.
Psalm 5:7

I will give Thee thanks in the great congregation: I will praise Thee among much people.   *Psalm 35:18*

Blessed are they that dwell in Thy house: they will be still praising thee. Selah.
Psalm 84:4

It is a good thing to give thanks unto the Lord, and to sing praises unto Thy name, O most High:

To shew forth Thy loving kindness in the morning, and Thy faithfulness every night.   *Psalm 92:1,2*

O come, let us worship and bow down: let us kneel before the Lord our maker.
Psalm 95:6

Make a joyful noise unto the Lord, all ye lands.

Serve the Lord with gladness: come before His presence with singing.

Know ye that the Lord He is God: it is He that hath made us, and not we ourselves; we are His people, and the sheep of His pasture.

Enter into His gates with thanksgiving,

and into His courts with praise: be thankful unto Him, and bless His name.
Psalm 100:1-4

Oh that men would praise the Lord for His goodness, and for His wonderful works to the children of men!

Let them exalt Him also in the congregation of the people, and praise Him in the assembly of the elders.
Psalm 107:8,32

I will worship toward Thy holy temple, and praise Thy name for Thy lovingkindness and for Thy truth: for Thou hast magnified Thy word above all Thy name. *Psalm 138:2*

Praise ye the Lord, Praise God in His sanctuary: praise Him in the firmament of His power.

Praise Him for His mighty acts: praise Him according to His excellent greatness.

Praise Him with the sound of the trumpet: praise Him with the psaltery and harp.

Praise Him with the timbrel and dance: praise Him with stringed instruments and organs.

Praise Him upon the loud cymbals: praise Him upon the high sounding cymbals.

Let every thing that hath breath praise the Lord. Praise ye the Lord. *Psalm 150:1-6*

Sing, O ye heavens; for the Lord hath done it: shout, ye lower parts of the earth: break forth into singing, ye mountains, O forest, and every tree therein: for the Lord hath redeemed Jacob, and glorified Himself in Israel. *Isaiah 44:23*

Then saith Jesus unto him, Get thee hence, satan: for it is written, Thou shalt worship the Lord thy God, and Him only shalt thou serve. *Matthew 4:10*

And Jesus answered and said unto him, Get thee behind me, satan: for it is written, Thou shalt worship the Lord thy God, and Him only shalt thou serve. *Luke 4:8*

But the hour cometh, and now is, when the true worshippers shall worship the Father in spirit and in truth: for the Father seeketh such to worship Him.

God is a Spirit: and they that worship Him must worship Him in spirit and in truth. *John 4:23,24*

Now we know that God hearth not sinners: but if any man be a worshipper of God, and doeth His will, him He heareth.
John 9:31

What is it then? I will pray with the spirit, and I will pray with the understanding also: I will sing with the spirit, and I will sing with the understanding also.
1 Corinthians 14:15

For we are the circumcision, which worship God in the spirit, and rejoice in Christ Jesus, and have no confidence in the flesh. *Philippians 3:3*

Continue in prayer, and watch in the same with thanksgiving; *Colossians 4:2*

I will therefore that men pray every where, lifting up holy hands, without wrath and doubting. *1 Timothy 2:8*

Ye also, as lively stones, are built up a spiritual house, an holy priesthood, to offer up spiritual sacrifices, acceptable to God by Jesus Christ. *1 Peter 2:5*

94

Prayer

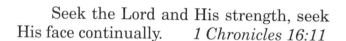

Seek the Lord and His strength, seek His face continually. *1 Chronicles 16:11*

If My people, which are called by My name, shall humble themselves, and pray, and seek My face, and turn from their wicked ways; then I will hear from Heaven, and will forgive their sin, and will heal their land.
2 Chronicles 7:14

When thou saidst, Seek ye My face; my heart said unto thee, Thy face, Lord, will I seek. *Psalm 27:8*

Yet the Lord will command His loving kindness in the daytime, and in the night His song shall be with me, and my prayer unto the God of my life. *Psalm 42:8*

As for me, I will call upon God; and the Lord shall save me.
Evening, and morning, and at noon, will

I pray, and cry aloud: and He shall hear my voice. *Psalm 55:16,17*

Glory ye in His holy name: let the heart of them rejoice that seek the Lord.
Seek the Lord, and His strength: seek His face evermore. *Psalm 105:3,4*

For my love they are my adversaries: but I give myself unto prayer. *Psalm 109:4*

The Lord is nigh unto all them that call upon Him, to all that call upon Him in truth. *Psalm 145:18*

Seek ye the Lord while He may be found, call ye upon Him while He is near: *Isaiah 55:6*

And all things, whatsoever ye shall ask in prayer, believing, ye shall receive. *Matthew 21:22*

Watch and pray, that ye enter not unto temptation: the spirit indeed is willing, but the flesh is weak. *Matthew 26:41*

And in the morning, rising up a great

while before day, He went out, and departed into a solitary place, and there prayed.
Mark 1:35

Therefore I say into you, What things soever ye desire, when ye pray, believe that ye receive them, and ye shall have them.
Mark 11:24

Take ye heed, watch and pray: for ye know not when the time is. *Mark 13:33*

And He spake a parable unto them to this end, that men ought always to pray, and not to faint; *Luke 18:1*

Watch ye therefore, and pray always, that ye may be accounted worthy to escape all these things that shall come to pass, and to stand before the Son of man. *Luke 21:36*

Likewise the Spirit also helpeth our infirmities: for we know not what we should pray for as we ought: but the Spirit itself maketh intercession for us with groanings which cannot be uttered. *Romans 8:26*

Rejoicing in hope; patient in tribulation;

continuing instant in prayer.
Romans 12:12

Praying always with all prayer and supplication in the Spirit, and watching thereunto with all perseverance and supplication for all saints; *Ephesians 6:18*

Pray without ceasing.
1 Thessalonians 5:17

I will therefore that men pray every where, lifting up holy hands, without wrath and doubting. *1 Timothy 2:8*

Let us therefore come boldly unto the throne of grace, that we may obtain mercy, and find grace to help in time of need.
Hebrews 4:16

But ye, beloved, building up yourselves on your most holy faith, praying in the Holy Ghost, *Jude 1:20*

95

PROTECTION

Happy art thou, O Israel: who is like unto thee, O people saved by the Lord, the shield of thy help, and Who is the sword of thy excellency! and thine enemies shall be found liars unto thee; and thou shalt tread upon their high places. *Deuteronomy 33:29*

And he said, The Lord is my rock, and my fortress, and my deliverer;
2 Samuel 22:2

Lord, how are they increased that trouble me! many are they that rise up against me. *Psalm 3:1*

But Thou, O Lord, art a shield for me; my glory, and the lifter up of mine head.
Psalm 3:3

In my distress I called upon the Lord, and cried unto my God: He heard my voice out of His temple, and my cry came before Him, even into His ears. *Psalm 18:6*

Thou hast also given me the shield of Thy salvation: and Thy right hand hath holden me up, and Thy gentleness hath made me great. *Psalm 18:35*

The Lord is my strength and my shield; my heart trusted in Him, and I am helped: therefore my heart greatly rejoiceth; and with my song will I praise Him. *Psalm 28:7*

The angel of the Lord encampeth round about them that fear Him, and delivereth them. *Psalm 34:7*

What time I am afraid, I will trust in Thee. *Psalm 56:3*

In God I will praise His word, in God I have put my trust; I will not fear what flesh can do unto me. *Psalm 56:4*

For the Lord God is a sun and a shield: the Lord will give grace and glory: no good thing will He withhold from them that walk uprightly. *Psalm 84:11*

He shall cover thee with His feathers, and under His wings shalt thou trust: His truth shall be thy shield and buckler.
Psalm 91:4

Ye that fear the Lord, trust in the Lord: He is their help and their shield.
Psalm 115:11

Thou art my hiding place and my shield: I hope in Thy word. *Psalm 119:114*

My goodness, and my fortress; my high tower, and my deliverer; my shield, and He in whom I trust; who subdueth my people under me. *Psalm 144:2*

Fear thou not; for I am with thee: be not dismayed; for I am thy God: I will strengthen thee: yea, I will help thee; yea, I will uphold thee with the right hand of My righteousness. *Isaiah 41:10*

For I the Lord thy God will hold thy right hand, saying unto thee, Fear not; I will help thee. *Isaiah 41:13*

Above all, taking the shield of faith, Wherewith ye shall be able to quench all the fiery darts of the wicked. *Ephesians 6:16*

What You Respect-
You Will Attract.

-MIKE MURDOCK

Copyright © 2001 by Mike Murdock • Wisdom International
The Wisdom Center • P.O. Box 99 • Denton, TX 76202

96

RESPECT

Trust in the Lord, and do good; so shalt thou dwell in the land, and verily thou shalt be fed. *Psalm 37:3*

The steps of a good man are ordered by the Lord: and he delighteth in His way.
Psalm 37:23

For the Lord God is a sun and shield: the Lord will give grace and glory: no good thing will He withhold from them that walk uprightly. *Psalm 84:11*

A good man leaveth an inheritance to his children's children: and the wealth of the sinner is laid up for the just.
Proverbs 13:22

A good name is rather to be chosen than great riches, and loving favour rather than silver and gold. *Proverbs 22:1*

A good name is better than precious ointment; and the day of death than the day of one's birth. *Ecclesiastes 7:1*

Let your light so shine before men, that they may see your good works, and glorify your Father which is in heaven.
Matthew 5:16

The disciple is not above his master, nor the servant above his lord. *Matthew 10:24*

A good man out of the good treasure of his heart bringeth forth that which is good; and an evil man out of the evil treasure of his heart bringeth forth that which is evil: for of the abundance of the heart his mouth speaketh. *Luke 6:45*

Let not then your good be evil spoken of: *Romans 14:16*

~ 97 ~

SELF-CONTROL

For wrath killeth the foolish man, and envy slayeth the silly one. *Job 5:2*

My lips shall not speak wickedness, nor my tongue utter deceit. *Job 27:4*

Deliver my soul, O Lord, from lying lips, and from a deceitful tongue. *Psalm 120:2*

What shall be given unto thee? or what shall be done unto thee, thou false tongues? *Psalm 120:3*

Set a watch, O Lord, before my mouth; keep the door of my lips. *Psalm 141:3*

The mouth of a righteous man is a well of life: but violence covereth the mouth of the wicked. *Proverbs 10:11*

In the multitude of words there wanteth not sin: but he that refraineth his lips is wise. *Proverbs 10:19*

A fool's wrath is presently known: but a prudent man covereth shame.
Proverbs 12:16

He that keepeth his mouth keepeth his life: but he that openeth wide his lips shall have destruction. *Proverbs 13:3*

He that is slow to wrath is of great understanding: but he that is hasty of spirit exalteth folly. *Proverbs 14:29*

Be not hasty in thy spirit to be angry: for anger resteth in the bosom of fools.
Ecclesiastes 7:9

But I say unto you, That every idle word that men shall speak, they shall give account thereof in the day of judgment.
Matthew 12:36

For by thy words thou shalt be justified, and by thy words thou shalt be condemned.
Matthew 12:37

Be ye angry, and sin not: let not the sun go down upon your wrath:
Ephesians 4:26

But now ye also put off all these; anger; wrath, malice, blasphemy, filthy communication out of your mouth.
Colossians 3:8

Wherefore, my beloved brethren, let every man be swift to hear, slow to speak, slow to wrath: *James 1:19*

For the wrath of man worketh not the righteousness of God. *James 1:20*

Even so the tongue is a little member, and boasteth great things. Behold, how great a matter a little fire kindleth! *James 3:5*

98

SERVANT'S HEART

Behold, as the eyes of servants look unto the hand of their masters, and as the eyes of a maiden unto the hand of her mistress; so our eyes wait upon the Lord our God, until that He have mercy upon us.   *Psalm 123:2*

As the cold of snow in the time of harvest, so is a faithful messenger to them that send him: for he refresheth the soul of his masters.   *Proverbs 25:13*

Whoso keepeth the fig tree shall eat the fruit thereof: so he that waiteth on his master shall be honoured.   *Proverbs 27:18*

And whosoever shall give to drink unto one of these little ones a cup of cold water only in the name of a disciple, verily I say unto you, he shall in no wise lose his reward.
Matthew 10:42

Even as the Son of man came not to be ministered unto, but to minister, and to give His life a ransom for many. *Matthew 20:28*

Who then is a faithful and wise servant, whom his lord hath made ruler over his household, to give them meat in due season?
Matthew 24:45

Blessed is that servant, whom his lord when he cometh shall find so doing.
Matthew 24:46

Verily I say unto you, That he shall make him ruler over all his goods.
Matthew 24:47

But so shall it not be among you: but whosoever will be great among you, shall be your minister. *Mark 10:43*

And whosoever of you will be the chiefest, shall be servant of all. *Mark 10:44*

Which now of these three, thinkest thou, was neighbour unto him that fell among the thieves? *Luke 10:36*

And the Lord said, Who then is that

faithful and wise steward, whom his lord shall make ruler over his household, to give them their portion of meat in due season?
Luke 12:42

No servant can serve two masters: for either he will hate the one, and love the other; or else he will hold to the one, and despise the other. Ye cannot serve God and mammon. *Luke 16:13*

For whether is greater, he that sitteth at meat, or he that serveth? is not he that sitteth at meat? but I am among you as he that serveth. *Luke 22:27*

Verily, verily, I say unto you, The servant is not greater than his lord; neither he that is sent greater than he that sent him.
John 13:16

Moreover it is required in stewards, that a man be found faithful.
1 Corinthians 4:2

Bear ye one another's burdens, and so fulfil the law of Christ. *Galatians 6:2*

As we have therefore opportunity, let us do good unto all men, especially unto them who are of the household of faith.

Galatians 6:10

Servants, be obedient to them that are your masters according to the flesh, with fear and trembling, in singleness of your heart, as unto Christ; *Ephesians 6:5*

With good will doing service, as to the Lord, and not to men: *Ephesians 6:7*

Servants, obey in all things your masters according to the flesh; not with eyeservice, as menpleasers; but in singleness of heart, fearing God: *Colossians 3:22*

Exhort servants to be obedient unto their own masters, and to please them well in all things; not answering again;

Titus 2:9

Servants, be subject to your masters with all fear; not only to the good and gentle, but also to the froward. *1 Peter 2:18*

99

STRENGTH

Then he said unto them, Go your way, eat the fat, and drink the sweet, and send portions unto them for whom nothing is prepared: for this day is holy unto our Lord: neither be ye sorry; for the joy of the Lord is your strength. *Nehemiah 8:10*

The Lord hear thee in the day of trouble; the name of the God of Jacob defend thee;
Psalm 20:1

Send thee help from the sanctuary, and strengthen thee out of Zion; *Psalm 20:2*

Wait on the Lord: be of good courage, and He shall strengthen thine heart: wait, I say, on the Lord. *Psalm 27:14*

Bow down thine ear to me; deliver me speedily: be Thou my strong rock, for an house of defence to save me. *Psalm 31:2*

Be of good courage, and He shall strengthen your heart, all ye that hope in the Lord. *Psalm 31:24*

Be Thou my strong habitation, whereunto I may continually resort: Thou hast given commandment to save me; for Thou art my rock and my fortress.
Psalm 71:3

My soul melteth for heaviness: strengthen Thou me according unto Thy word. *Psalm 119:28*

In the day when I cried Thou answeredst me, and strengthenedst me with strength in my soul. *Psalm 138:3*

The way of the Lord is strength to the upright: but destruction shall be to the workers of iniquity. *Proverbs 10:29*

In the fear of the Lord is strong confidence: and His children shall have a place of refuge. *Proverbs 14:26*

Behold, God is my salvation; I will trust, and not be afraid: for the Lord Jehovah is my strength and my song; He also is become my salvation. *Isaiah 12:2*

He giveth power to the faint; and to them that have no might He increaseth strength. *Isaiah 40:29*

But they that wait upon the Lord shall renew their strength; they shall mount up with wings as eagles; they shall run, and not be weary; and they shall walk, and not faint.
Isaiah 40:31

Fear thou not; for I am with thee; be not dismayed; for I am thy God: I will strengthen thee; yea, I will help thee; yea, I will uphold thee with the right hand of My righteousness. *Isaiah 41:10*

And said, O man greatly beloved, fear not: peace be unto thee, be strong, yea, be strong. And when He had spoken unto me, I was strengthened, and said, Let my Lord speak; for Thou hast strengthened me.
Daniel 10:19

The Lord God is my strength, and He will make my feet like hinds' feet, and He will make me to walk upon mine high places. To the chief singer on my stringed instruments. *Habakkuk 3:19*

Therefore I take pleasure in infirmities, in reproaches, in necessities, in persecutions, in distresses for Christ's sake: for when I am weak, then am I strong.
2 Corinthians 12:10

That He would grant you, according to the riches of His glory, to be strengthened with might by His Spirit in the inner man;
Ephesians 3:16

I can do all things through Christ which strengtheneth me. *Philippians 4:13*

100

Wisdom

Give therefore thy servant an understanding heart to judge thy people, that I may discern between good and bad: for who is able to judge this Thy so great a people? *1 Kings 3:9*

I will bless the Lord, who hath given me counsel: my reins also instruct me in the night seasons. *Psalm 16:7*

Teach me Thy way, O Lord, and lead me in a plain path, because of mine enemies. *Psalm 27:11*

Lord, make me to know mine end, and the measure of my days, what it is; that I may know how frail I am. *Psalm 39:4*

O send out Thy light and Thy truth: let them lead me; let them bring me unto Thy holy hill, and to Thy tabernacles. *Psalm 43:3*

So teach us to number our days, that we may apply our hearts unto wisdom.
Psalm 90:12

I am Thy servant; give me understanding, that I may know Thy testimonies. *Psalm 119:125*

The entrance of Thy words giveth light; it giveth understanding unto the simple.
Psalm 119:130

For the Lord giveth wisdom: out of His mouth cometh knowledge and understanding. *Proverbs 2:6*

He layeth up sound wisdom for the righteous: He is a buckler to them that walk uprightly. *Proverbs 2:7*

In all thy ways acknowledge Him, and He shall direct thy paths. *Proverbs 3:6*

For God giveth to a man that is good in His sight wisdom, and knowledge, and joy: but to the sinner He giveth travail, to gather and to heap up, that He may give to him that is good before God. This also is vanity and vexation of spirit. *Ecclesiastes 2:26*

And thine ears shall hear a word behind thee, saying, This is the way, walk ye in it, when ye turn to the right hand, and when ye turn to the left. *Isaiah 30:21*

For I will give you a mouth and wisdom, which all your adversaries shall not be able to gainsay nor resist. *Luke 21:15*

Howbeit when He, the Spirit of truth, is come, He will guide you into all truth: for He shall not speak of Himself; but whatsoever He shall hear, that shall He speak: and He will shew you things to come. *John 16:13*

He shall glorify Me: for he shall receive of Mine, and shall shew it unto you. *John 16:14*

For to one is given by the Spirit the word of wisdom; to another the word of knowledge by the same Spirit; *1 Corinthians 12:8*

That the God of our Lord Jesus Christ, the Father of glory, may give unto you the spirit of wisdom and revelation in the knowledge of Him: *Ephesians 1:17*

The eyes of your understanding being enlightened; that ye may know what is the hope of His calling, and what the riches of the glory of His inheritance in the saints,
Ephesians 1:18

For this cause we also, since the day we heard it, do not cease to pray for you, and to desire that ye might be filled with the knowledge of His will in all wisdom and spiritual understanding; *Colossians 1:9*

That ye might walk worthy of the Lord unto all pleasing, being fruitful in every good work, and increasing in the knowledge of God; *Colossians 1:10*

For God hath not given us the spirit of fear; but of power, and of love, and of a sound mind. *2 Timothy 1:7*

If any of you lack wisdom, let him ask of God, that giveth to all men liberally, and upbraideth not; and it shall be given him.
James 1:5

101

WORD OF GOD

And these words, which I command thee this day, shall be in thine heart:
Deuteronomy 6:6

The secret things belong unto the Lord our God: but those things which are revealed belong unto us and to our children for ever, that we may do all the words of this law.
Deuteronomy 29:29

But the word is very nigh unto thee, in thy mouth, and in thy heart, that thou mayest do it. *Deuteronomy 30:14*

This book of the law shall not depart out of thy mouth; but thou shalt meditate therein day and night, that thou mayest observe to do according to all that is written therein: for then thou shalt make thy way prosperous, and then thou shalt have good success. *Joshua 1:8*

Be ye mindful always of His covenant; the word which He commanded to a thousand generations; *1 Chronicles 16:15*

Receive, I pray thee, the law from His mouth, and lay up His words in thine heart. *Job 22:22*

Neither have I gone back from the commandment of His lips; I have esteemed the words of His mouth more than my necessary food. *Job 23:12*

Blessed is the man that walketh not in the counsel of the ungodly, nor standeth in the way of sinners, nor sitteth in the seat of the scornful.
But his delight is in the law of the Lord; and in His law doth he meditate day and night. *Psalm 1:1,2*

The law of the Lord is perfect, converting the soul: the testimony of the Lord is sure, making wise the simple.
Psalm 19:7

For Thou art my rock and my fortress; therefore for Thy name's sake lead me, and guide me. *Psalm 31:3*

I will instruct thee and teach thee in the way which thou shalt go: I will guide thee with Mine eye. *Psalm 32:8*

The law of his God is in his heart; none of his steps shall slide. *Psalm 37:31*

Wherewithal shall a young man cleanse his way? by taking heed thereto according to Thy word.
Thy word have I hid in mine heart, that I might not sin against Thee.
Thy word is a lamp unto my feet, and a light into my path. *Psalm 119:9,11,105*

When thou goest, it shall lead thee; when thou sleepest, it shall keep thee; and when thou awakest, it shall talk with thee.
For the commandment is a lamp; and the law is light; and reproofs of instruction are the way of life: *Proverbs 6:22,23*

Commit thy works unto the Lord, and thy thoughts shall be established.
Proverbs 16:3

And thine ears shall hear a word behind thee, saying, This is the way, walk ye in it, when ye turn to the right hand, and when ye turn to the left. *Isaiah 30:21*

The grass withereth, the flower fadeth: but the word of our God shall stand for ever. *Isaiah 40:8*

Therefore whosoever heareth these sayings of Mine, and doeth them, I will liken him unto a wise man, which built his house upon a rock: *Matthew 7:24*

Jesus answered and said unto them, Ye do err, not knowing the scriptures, nor the power of God. *Matthew 22:29*

Heaven and earth shall pass away: but My words shall not pass away. *Mark 13:31*

Search the scriptures; for in them ye think ye have eternal life: and they are they which testify of Me. *John 5:39*

Then said Jesus to those Jews which believed on Him, If ye continue in My word, then are ye My disciples indeed;
And ye shall know the truth, and the truth shall make you free. *John 8:31,32*

So then faith cometh by hearing, and hearing by the word of God. *Romans 10:17*

All scripture is given by inspiration of God, and is profitable for doctrine, for reproof, for correction, for instruction in righteousness:

That the man of God may be perfect, throughly furnished unto all good works.
2 Timothy 3:16,17

Whereby are given unto us exceeding great and precious promises: that by these ye might be partakers of the divine nature, having escaped the corruption that is in the world through lust.

For the prophecy came not in old time by the will of man: but holy men of God spake as they were moved by the Holy Ghost.
2 Peter 1:4,21

101 Wisdom Keys

1. Never Complain About What You Permit.
2. The Problem That Infuriates You The Most Is The Problem That God Has Assigned You To Solve.
3. Those Who Unlock Your Compassion Are Those To Whom You Have Been Assigned.
4. What You Are Willing To Walk Away From Determines What God Will Bring To You.
5. The Secret Of Your Future Is Hidden In Your Daily Routine.
6. Your Rewards In Life Are Determined By The Problems You Solve For Others.
7. When You Want Something You Have Never Had, You Have Got To Do Something You Have Never Done.
8. All Men Fall...The Great Ones Get Back Up.
9. Intolerance Of Your Present Creates Your Future.
10. Those Who Cannot Increase You Will Inevitably Decrease You.
11. You Will Never Leave Where You Are Until You Decide Where You Would Rather Be.
12. You Will Only Have Significant Success With Something That Is An Obsession.
13. Give Another What He Cannot Find Anywhere Else And He Will Keep Returning.
14. Your Assignment Is Not Your Decision But Your Discovery.
15. When Fatigue Walks In, Faith Walks Out.

16. If What You Hold In Your Hand Is Not Enough To Be Your Harvest, Make It Your Seed.
17. You Will Never Change What You Believe Until Your Belief System Cannot Produce Something You Want.
18. You Will Only Be Pursued For The Problems You Solve.
19. Champions Are Willing To Do Things They Hate To Create Something They Love.
20. You Will Never Possess What You Are Unwilling To Pursue.
21. The Only Reason Men Fail Is Broken Focus.
22. Stop Looking At Where You Have Been And Start Looking At Where You Can Be.
23. You Will Only Be Remembered For Two Things; The Problems You Solve Or The Ones You Create.
24. Those Who Transfer Knowledge Are Also Capable Of Transferring Error.
25. Your Seed Is The Only Influence You Have Over Your Future.
26. Loneliness Is Not The Absence Of Affection, But The Absence Of Direction.
27. You Cannot Be What You Are Not, But You Can Become What You Are Not.
28. False Accusation Is The Last Stage Before Supernatural Promotion.
29. Your Seed Is A Photograph Of Your Faith.
30. What You Repeatedly Hear You Will Eventually Believe.
31. God Never Consults Your Past To Determine Your Future.

32. Satan Always Attacks Those Next In Line For A Promotion.
33. Power Is The Ability To Walk Away From Something You Desire...To Protect Something You Love.
34. Anything That Does Not Change You Is Unnecessary In Your Life.
35. When You Discover Your Assignment, You Will Discover Your Enemy.
36. What You Respect, You Will Attract.
37. Men Decide Their Habits...Their Habits Decide Their Future.
38. You Cannot Correct What You Are Unwilling To Confront.
39. The Proof Of Desire Is Pursuit.
40. Crisis Always Occurs At The Curve Of Change.
41. If Time Heals, God Is Unnecessary.
42. Your Seed Is Anything That Benefits Another While Your Harvest Is Anything That Benefits You.
43. Satan's Favorite Entry Point Into Your Life Is Always Through Someone Close To You.
44. What You Hate Reveals What You Were Created To Correct.
45. Losers Focus On What They Are Going Through While Champions Focus On What They Are Going To.
46. When You Let Go Of What Is In Your Hand, God Will Let Go Of What Is In His Hand.
47. Pain Is Not An Enemy But Merely The Proof That One Exists.

48. When God Wants To Bless You, He Puts A Person In Your Life...When Satan Wants To Destroy You, He Puts A Person In Your Life.
49. Currents Of Favor Begin To Flow The Moment You Solve A Problem For Someone.
50. The Seed That Leaves Your Hand Never Leaves Your Life...But Enters Your Future, Where It Multiplies.
51. Each Act Of Obedience Shortens The Distance To Any Miracle You Are Pursuing.
52. The Quality Of Your Preparation Determines The Quality Of Your Performance.
53. Champions Make Decisions That Create The Future They Desire...Losers Make Decisions That Create The Present They Desire.
54. Creativity Is The Search For Options; Concentration Is The Elimination Of Them.
55. Seed-Faith Is Sowing What You Have Been Given...To Create What You Have Been Promised.
56. The Seasons Of Your Life Will Change Every Time You Decide To Use Your Faith.
57. Someone Is Always Observing You Who Is Capable Of Greatly Blessing You.
58. Giving Is Proof That You Have Conquered Greed.
59. The Season For Research Is Not The Season For Marketing.

60. What You Fail To Master In Your Life Will Eventually Master You.
61. Go Where You Are Celebrated Instead Of Where You Are Tolerated.
62. The Broken Become Masters At Mending.
63. Your Significance Is Not In Your Similarity To Another, But In Your Point Of Difference From Another.
64. You Will Always Pursue The Friendship That Solves Your Most Immediate Problem.
65. The Worth Of Any Relationship Can Be Measured By Its Contributions To Your Priorities.
66. You Will Never Conquer What You Refuse To Hate.
67. Injustice Is Only As Powerful As Your Memory Of It.
68. Every Relationship In Your Life Is A Current Moving You Toward Your Dreams Or Away From Them.
69. You Will Never Be Promoted Until You Have Become Over-Qualified For Your Present Assignment.
70. Money Is Merely A Reward For Solving Problems.
71. Your Reaction To Someone In Trouble Determines God's Reaction To You The Next Time You Get In Trouble.
72. What You Can Tolerate, You Cannot Change.

73. The Waves Of Yesterday's Disobedience Will Splash On The Shores Of Today For A Season.
74. You Will Never Outgrow Warfare...You Must Simply Learn To Fight.
75. Nothing Is Ever As Bad As it First Appears.
76. The Evidence Of God's Presence Far Outweighs The Proof Of His Absence.
77. Patience Is The Weapon That Forces Deception To Reveal Itself.
78. One Hour In The Presence Of God Will Reveal Any Flaw In Your Most Carefully Laid Plan.
79. Never Spend More Time On A Critic Than You Would Give To A Friend.
80. Those Who Do Not Respect Your Assignment Disqualify Themselves For A Relationship.
81. You Will Never Reach The Palace Talking Like A Peasant.
82. Struggle Is The Proof You Have Not Yet Been Conquered.
83. Never Discuss Your Problem With Someone Incapable Of Solving It.
84. Greatness Is Not The Pursuit Of Perfection But The Pursuit Of Completion.
85. Never Rewrite Your Theology To Accommodate A Tragedy.
86. The Greatest Quality On Earth Is The Willingness To Become.

87. Warfare Always Surrounds The Birth Of A Miracle.
88. Failure Is Not An Event, But An Opinion.
89. You Are Never As Far From A Miracle As It First Appears.
90. What You See Determines What You Desire.
91. The Atmosphere You Permit Determines The Product You Produce.
92. Prosperity Is Simply Having Enough Of God's Provision To Complete His Instructions For Your Life.
93. God Will Never Advance Your Instructions Beyond Your Last Act Of Disobedience.
94. Anger Is The Birthplace For Solution.
95. Those Who Do Not Respect Your Time Will Not Respect Your Wisdom Either.
96. Discontent Is The Catalyst For Change.
97. Crisis Is Merely Concentrated Information.
98. Silence Cannot Be Misquoted.
99. Those Who Created The Pain Of Yesterday Do Not Control The Pleasure Of Tomorrow.
100. When You Change Your Focus You Will Change Your Feelings.
101. What You Make Happen For Others, God Will Make Happen For You.

31 Facts About Wisdom

1. Wisdom Is The Master Key To All The Treasures Of Life. (2 Chronicles 1:7,8,10-12; Colossians 2:2,3)
2. Wisdom Is A Gift From God To You. (Proverbs 2:6; Daniel 2:21; 1 Corinthians 12:8)
3. The Fear Of God Is The Beginning Of Wisdom. (Job 28:28; Psalm 111:10; Proverbs 9:10)
4. The Wisdom Of This World Is A False Substitute For The Wisdom Of God. (1 Corinthians 2:4,13; James 3:13-17)
5. The Wisdom Of Man Is Foolishness To God. (1 Corinthians 1:20,21,25; 1 Corinthians 3:19)
6. Right Relationships Increase Your Wisdom. (Proverbs 13:20; 1 Corinthians 15:33; 2 Thessalonians 3:6; 1 Timothy 6:5)
7. The Wisdom Of God Is Foolishness To The Natural Mind. (Proverbs 18:2; Isaiah 55:8,9; 1 Corinthians 2:4,5)
8. Your Conversation Reveals How Much Wisdom You Possess. (1 Kings 10:24; Proverbs 18:21; Proverbs 29:11; James 3:2)

9. Jesus Is Made Unto Us Wisdom. (1 Corinthians 1:30; Ephesians 1:5,8,17)
10. All The Treasures Of Wisdom And Knowledge Are Hid In Jesus Christ. (1 Corinthians 1:23,24; 1 Corinthians 2:7,8; Colossians 2:2,3)
11. The Word Of God Is Your Source Of Wisdom. (Deuteronomy 4:5,6; Psalm 119:98-100; Proverbs 2:6)
12. God Will Give You Wisdom When You Take The Time To Listen. (Proverbs 2:6; Isaiah 40:31; John 10:27; James 1:5)
13. The Word Of God Is Able To Make You Wise Unto Salvation. (Psalm 107:43; John 5:39)
14. The Holy Spirit Is The Spirit Of Wisdom That Unleashes Your Gifts, Talents And Skills. (Exodus 31:1,3,4; Exodus 36:1; Daniel 1:4)
15. Men Of Wisdom Will Always Be Men Of Mercy. (Galatians 6:1; James 3:17; James 5:19,20)
16. Wisdom Is Better Than Jewels Or Money. (Job 28:18; Proverbs 3:13-15; Proverbs 8:11; Proverbs 16:16)
17. Wisdom Is More Powerful Than Weapons Of War. (Proverbs 12:6; Ecclesiastes 9:18; Isaiah 33:6; Acts 6:10)
18. He That Wins Souls Is Wise. (Proverbs 11:30; Daniel 12:3; Romans 10:14,15)

19. The Wise Hate Evil And The Evil Hate The Wise. (Proverbs 1:7,22; Proverbs 8:13; Proverbs 9:8; Proverbs 18:2)
20. Wisdom Reveals The Treasure In Yourself. (Proverbs 19:8; Ephesians 2:10; Philippians 1:6; 1 Peter 2:9,10)
21. The Proof Of Wisdom Is The Presence Of Joy And Peace. (Psalm 119:165; Proverbs 3:13; Ecclesiastes 7:12; James 3:17)
22. Wisdom Makes Your Enemies Helpless Against You. (Proverbs 16:7; Ecclesiastes 7:12; Isaiah 54:17; Luke 21:15)
23. Wisdom Creates Currents Of Favor And Recognition Toward You. (Proverbs 3:1-4; Proverbs 4:8; Proverbs 8:34,35)
24. The Wise Welcome Correction. (Proverbs 3:11,12; Proverbs 9:8,9)
25. When The Wise Speak, Healing Flows. (Proverbs 10:11,20,21; Proverbs 12:18)
26. When You Increase Your Wisdom You Will Increase Your Wealth. (Psalm 112:1-3; Proverbs 3:16; Proverbs 8:18-21; Proverbs 14:24)
27. Wisdom Can Be Imparted By The Laying On Of Hands Of A Man Of God. (Deuteronomy 34:9; Acts 6:6-8,10; 2 Timothy 1:6,14)

28. Wisdom Guarantees Promotion. (Proverbs 4:8,9; Proverbs 8:15,16; Ezra 7:25)
29. Wisdom Loves Those Who Love Her. (Proverbs 2:3-5; Proverbs 8:17,21)
30. Wisdom Will Be Given To You When You Pray For It In Faith. (Matthew 7:7,8,11; James 1:5,6)
31. The Mantle Of Wisdom Makes You Ten Times Stronger Than Those Without It. (Psalm 91:7; Ecclesiastes 7:19; Daniel 1:17,20)

JOIN THE
Wisdom Key 3000 TODAY!

Dear Partner,

God has connected us!

I have asked the Holy Spirit for 3000 Special Partners who will plant a monthly Seed of $58.00 to help me bring the gospel around the world. (58 represents 58 kinds of blessing in the Bible.)

Will you become my monthly Faith Partner in The Wisdom Key 3000? Your monthly Seed of $58.00 is so powerful in helping heal broken lives. When you sow into the work of God, 4 Miracle Harvests are guaranteed in Scripture:

- ▶ Uncommon Protection (Mal. 3:10,11)
- ▶ Uncommon Favor (Lk. 6:38)
- ▶ Uncommon Health (Isa. 58:8)
- ▶ Financial Ideas and Wisdom (Deut. 8:18)

Your Faith Partner,

Mike Murdock

☐ **Yes Mike, I want to join The Wisdom Key 3000. Enclosed is my monthly Seed-Faith Promise of ☐ $58 ☐ Other $_____. Please rush The Wisdom Key Partnership Pak to me today!**

☐ CHECK ☐ MONEY ORDER ☐ AMEX ☐ DISCOVER ☐ MASTERCARD ☐ VIS

Credit Card # _____ Exp. ___/___

Signature _____

Name _____ Birth Date ___/___/___

Address _____

City _____ State _____ Zip _____

Phone _____ E-Mail _____

Your Seed-Faith offerings are used to support the Mike Murdock Evangelistic Association, The Wisdom Center and all its programs. The Mini reserves the right to redirect funds as needed in order to carry out our charitable purpose.

Clip and mail completed form to:

THE WISDOM CENTER
P.O. Box 99, Denton, Texas 76202

1-888-WISDOM1
(1-888-947-3661)

Website:
WWW.THEWISDOMCENTER.TV

Clip and Mail

DECISION

Will You Accept Jesus As Your Personal Savior Today?

The Bible says, "That if thou shalt confess with thy mouth the Lord Jesus, and shalt believe in thine heart that God hath raised Him from the dead, thou shalt be saved" (Romans 10:9).

Pray this prayer from your heart today! *"Dear Jesus, I believe that You died for me and rose again on the third day. I confess I am a sinner...I need Your love and forgiveness...Come into my heart. Forgive my sins. I receive Your eternal life. Confirm Your love by giving me peace, joy and supernatural love for others. Amen."*

DR. MIKE MURDOCK

is in tremendous demand as one of the most dynamic speakers in America today.

More than 14,000 audiences in 38 countries have attended his Schools of Wisdom. Hundreds of invitations come to him from churches, colleges and business corporations. He is a noted author of over 130 books, including the best sellers, *"The Leadership Secrets of Jesus"* and *"Secrets of the Richest Man Who Ever Lived."* Thousands view his weekly television program, *"Wisdom Keys with Mike Murdock."* Many attend his Saturday School of Wisdom Breakfasts that he hosts in major cities of America.

☐ Yes, Mike! I made a decision to accept Christ as my personal Savior today. Please send me my free gift of your book *"31 Keys to a New Beginning"* to help me with my new life in Christ. *(B-48)*

Name_____ Birthdate___/___

Address_____

City_____ State_____ Zip_____

Phone (___)_____ E-Mail_____

Mail To: *(B-33)*
The Wisdom Center · P.O. Box 99 · Denton, TX 76202
1-888-WISDOM-1 (1-888-947-3661)
Website: www.thewisdomcenter.tv

ABOUT *MIKE MURDOCK*

- Has embraced his Assignment to pursue...possess...and publish the Wisdom of God to help people achieve their dreams and goals.

- Began full-time evangelism at the age of 19, which has continued since 1966.

- Has traveled and spoken to more than 14,000 audiences in 38 countries, including East and West Africa, the Orient and Europe.

- Noted author of over 130 books, including best sellers, *"Wisdom For Winning," "Dream Seeds"* and *"The Double Diamond Principle."*

- Created the popular *"Topical Bible"* series for Businessmen, Mothers, Fathers, Teenagers, and the *"One-Minute Pocket Bible"* series and *"The Uncommon Life"* series.

- Has composed more than 5,700 songs such as *"I Am Blessed," "You Can Make It," "Holy Spirit This Is Your House"* and *"Jesus, Just The Mention Of Your Name,"* recorded by many gospel artists.

- Is the Founder of The Wisdom Center, in Denton Texas.

- Has a weekly television program called *"Wisdom Keys With Mike Murdock."*

- Has appeared often on TBN, CBN, BET and other television network programs.

- Is a Founding Trustee on the Board of Charismatic Bible Ministries with Oral Roberts.

- Has had more than 3,500 accept the call into full-time ministry under his ministry.

SCHOOL of WISDOM #2

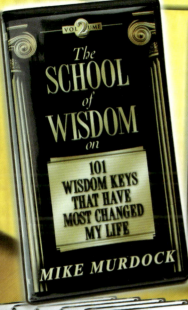

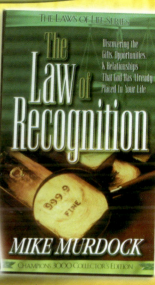

- 47 Keys In Recognizing The Mate God Has Approved For You
- 14 Facts You Should Know About Your Gifts And Talents
- 17 Important Facts You Should Remember About Your Weakness
- And Much, Much More...

- What Attracts Others Toward You
- The Secret Of Multiplying Your Financial Blessings
- What Stops The Flow Of Your Faith
- Why Some Fail And Others Succeed
- How To Discern Your Life Assignment
- How To Create Currents Of Favor With Others
- How To Defeat Loneliness

The Wisdom Center
6 Tapes | $30
PAK-002
Wisdom Is The Principal Thing

The Wisdom Center
Free Book
B-114 ($10 Value)
ENCLOSED!
Wisdom Is The Principal Thing

Add 10% For S/H

THE WISDOM CENTER
P.O. Box 99, Denton, Texas 76202

1-888-WISDOM1
(1-888-947-3661)

Website:
WWW.THEWISDOMCENTER.TV

A

Financial Success.

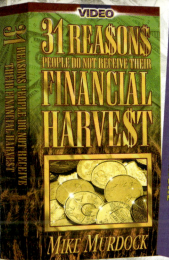
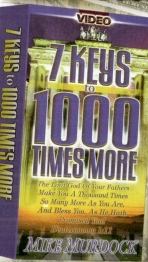

- **8 Scriptural Reasons You Should Pursue Financial Prosperity**
- **The Secret Prayer Key You Need When Making A Financial Request To God**
- **The Weapon Of Expectation And The 5 Miracles It Unlocks**
- **How To Discern Those Who Qualify To Receive Your Financial Assistance**
- **How To Predict The Miracle Moment God Will Schedule Your Financial Breakthrough**
- **Habits Of Uncommon Achievers**
- **The Greatest Success Law I Ever Discovered**
- **How To Discern Your Place Of Assignment, The Only Place Financial Provision Is Guaranteed**
- **3 Secret Keys In Solving Problems For Others**

The Wisdom Center
Video Pak AMVIDEO | **$30**
Buy 1-Get 1 Free
(A $60 Value!)
Wisdom Is The Principal Thing

Add 10% For S/H

THE WISDOM CENTER
P.O. Box 99, Denton, Texas 76202

1-888-WISDOM1
(1-888-947-3661)

Website:
WWW.THEWISDOMCENTER.TV

Songs From The Secret Place!

The Music Ministry of MIKE MURDOCK

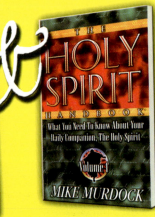

The Wisdom Center
6 Tapes | $30
PAK-007
Wisdom Is The Principal Thing

Free Book
B-100 ($10 Value)
ENCLOSED!
Wisdom Is The Principal Thing

Songs...

1. A Holy Place
2. Anything You Want
3. Everything Comes From You
4. Fill This Place With Your Presence
5. First Thing Every Morning
6. Holy Spirit, I Want To Hear You
7. Holy Spirit, Move Again
8. Holy Spirit, You Are Enough
9. I Don't Know What I Would Do Without You
10. I Let Go (Of Anything That Stops Me)
11. I'll Just Fall On You
12. I Love You, Holy Spirit
13. I'm Building My Life Around You
14. I'm Giving Myself To You
15. I'm In Love! I'm In Love!
16. I Need Water (Holy Spirit, You're My Well)
17. In The Secret Place
18. In Your Presence, I'm Always Changed
19. In Your Presence (Miracles Are Born)
20. I've Got To Live In Your Presence
21. I Want To Hear Your Voice
22. I Will Do Things Your Way
23. Just One Day At A Time
24. Meet Me In The Secret Place
25. More Than Ever Before
26. Nobody Else Does What You Do
27. No No Walls!
28. Nothing Else Matters Anymore (Since I've Been In The Presence Of You Lord)
29. Nowhere Else
30. Once Again You've Answered
31. Only A Fool Would Try (To Live Without You)
32. Take Me Now
33. Teach Me How To Please You
34. There's No Place I'd Rather Be
35. Thy Word Is All That Matters
36. When I Get In Your Presence
37. You're The Best Thing (That's Ever Happened To Me)
38. You Are Wonderful
39. You've Done It Once
40. You Keep Changing Me
41. You Satisfy

Add 10% For S/H

THE WISDOM CENTER
P.O. Box 99, Denton, Texas 76202
1-888-WISDOM1
(1-888-947-3661)
Website:
WWW.THEWISDOMCENTER.TV

The Uncommon Woman

- Master Keys In Understanding The Man In Your Life
- The One Thing Every Man Attempts To Move Away From
- The Dominant Difference Between A Wrong Woman And A Right Woman
- What Causes Men To Withdraw

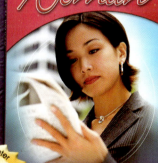

The Wisdom Center
6 Tapes | $30
PAK-009
Wisdom Is The Principal Thing

Free Book Enclosed!
B-49
Wisdom Is The Principal Thing

Add 10% For S/H

THE WISDOM CENTER
P.O. Box 99, Denton, Texas 76202

1-888-WISDOM1
(1-888-947-3661)

Website:
WWW.THEWISDOMCENTER.TV

E

UNCOMMON WISDOM FOR AN UNCOMMON MINISTRY

FOR *Ministers* ONLY!

Volume 1	B-1...
Volume 2	B-1...
Volume 3	B-1...
Volume 4	B-1...
Volume 5	B-1...
Volume 6	B-1...
Volume 7	B-1...

The Wisdom Center
7 Books for Only $20
$35 VALUE
PAKUM-1
Wisdom Is The Principal Thing

When God wants to touch a nation, He raises up a preacher. It is Uncommon Men and Women of God who have driven back the darkness and shielded the unlearned and rebellious from devastation by satanic forces. They offer the breath of life to a dead world. They open Golden Doors to Change. They unleash Forces of Truth in an age of deception.

An Uncommon Minister is prepared through seasons of pain, encounters with God, a... mentors. Having sat at the feet of Uncommon Mentors his entire life, Dr. Mike Murdock shar... practical but personal keys to increase the excellence and productivity of your ministry. Ea... volume of "The Uncommon Minister" is handy, convenient and easy to read. Your load will... lighter, your journey happier, and your effectiveness increased in "doing the will of the Father...

Add 10% For S/H

F | **THE WISDOM CENTER** P.O. Box 99, Denton, Texas 76202 | **1-888-WISDOM1** (1-888-947-3661) | Website: WWW.THEWISDOMCENTER.TV

What Every Parent Has Been Waiting For...

**A 12-Month Family Mentorship Program.
Over 365 Chapters Of Wisdom For Every Day Of The Year.**

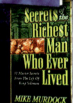

- 31 Keys To A New Beginning
- 31 Facts About Wisdom
- 31 Secrets of an Unforgettable Woman
- The Holy Spirit Handbook
- The Assignment: Volumes 1-4
- 31 Reasons People Do Not Receive Their Financial Harvest
- Secrets of The Richest Man Who Ever Lived
- The 3 Most Important Things In Your Life
- 31 Secrets To Career Success

**The Wisdom Center
Only $89
WBL-16 / $111 Value
Wisdom Is The Principal Thing**

Add 10% For S/H

THE WISDOM CENTER
P.O. Box 99, Denton, Texas 76202
1-888-WISDOM1
(1-888-947-3661)
Website:
WWW.THEWISDOMCENTER.TV

G

Book Store SPECIAL!

$1,985.00
A 40% Discount!
Plus
A 72" Book Rack Display FREE!

The Wisdom Center *Book Display* is available at last!

YOUR WHOLESALE PRICE
Your price for these 445 Wisdom Books (42 different titles) is only $1,985.00 ...a 40% discount. (Retail value of Books and Display Stand is $3,674.00)

FREE BOOK DISPLAY
Beautiful wood grain 72" Book Rack...holding up to 48 titles! It is a square, revolving Book Rack with clear plastic book shelves. The base is on casters for easy mobility...only 18" of floor space!

ORDER TODAY!
When you order today, The Wisdom Center will include this splendid 72" *Book Display* Book Rack for No Additional Cost!

WBD-72

Shipping cost of entire display and book an additional...$199.00

To place your order, contact:

H THE WISDOM CENTER
P.O. Box 99, Denton, Texas 76202
1-888-WISDOM1
(1-888-947-3661)
Website:
WWW.THEWISDOMCENTER.TV

The Wisdom Center *Book Display* (72")

THE WISDOM CENTER BOOK DISPLAY CONTAINS 445 BOOKS!

Slot #	Item #	Title Of Books	Quantity	Retail Cost Per Book	Total Retail Value
1	B-01	Wisdom For Winning	5	$10.00 ea	$50.00
2	B-01	Wisdom For Winning	5	$10.00 ea	$50.00
3	B-11	Dream Seeds	12	$9.00 ea	$108.00
4	B-26	The God Book	7	$10.00 ea	$70.00
5	B-27	The Jesus Book	7	$10.00 ea	$70.00
6	B-28	The Blessing Bible	6	$10.00 ea	$60.00
7	B-29	The Survival Bible	6	$10.00 ea	$60.00
8	B-40	Wisdom For Crisis Times	9	$9.00 ea	$81.00
9	B-42	One-Minute Businessman's Devotional	5	$12.00 ea	$60.00
10	B-43	One-Minute Businesswoman's Devotional	5	$12.00 ea	$60.00
11	B-44	31 Secrets For Career Success	9	$10.00 ea	$90.00
12	B-45	101 Wisdom Keys	17	$5.00 ea	$85.00
13	B-46	31 Facts About Wisdom	15	$5.00 ea	$75.00
14	B-47	Covenant Of Fifty-Eight Blessings	10	$8.00 ea	$80.00
15	B-48	31 Keys To A New Beginning	15	$5.00 ea	$75.00
16	B-49	The Proverbs 31 Woman	13	$7.00 ea	$91.00
17	B-54	31 Greatest Chapters In The Bible	5	$10.00 ea	$50.00
18	B-57	31 Secrets Of An Unforgettable Woman	8	$9.00 ea	$72.00
19	B-71	Wisdom: God's Golden Key To Success	11	$7.00 ea	$77.00
20	B-72	Double Diamond Daily Devotional	3	$15.00 ea	$45.00
21	B-74	The Assignment Vol. 1: The Dream And The Destiny	8	$10.00 ea	$80.00
22	B-75	The Assignment Vol. 2: The Anointing And The Adversity	7	$10.00 ea	$70.00
23	B-82	31 Reasons People Do Not Receive Their Financial Harvest	5	$12.00 ea	$60.00
24	B-82	31 Reasons People Do Not Receive Their Financial Harvest	5	$12.00 ea	$60.00
25	B-91	The Leadership Secrets Of Jesus	6	$10.00 ea	$60.00
26	B-91	The Leadership Secrets Of Jesus	6	$10.00 ea	$60.00
27	B-92	Secrets Of Journey Vol. 1	15	$5.00 ea	$75.00
28	B-93	Secrets Of Journey Vol. 2	15	$5.00 ea	$75.00
29	B-97	The Assignment Vol. 3: The Trials And The Triumph	7	$10.00 ea	$70.00
30	B-98	The Assignment Vol. 4: The Pain And The Passion	7	$10.00 ea	$70.00
31	B-99	Secrets Of The Richest Man Who Ever Lived	6	$10.00 ea	$60.00
32	B-99	Secrets Of The Richest Man Who Ever Lived	6	$10.00 ea	$60.00
33	B-100	Holy Spirit Handbook Vol. 1	8	$10.00 ea	$80.00
34	B-101	The 3 Most Important Things In Your Life	5	$10.00 ea	$50.00
35	B-101	The 3 Most Important Things In Your Life	5	$10.00 ea	$50.00
36	B-104	7 Keys To 1000 Times More	8	$10.00 ea	$80.00
37	B-104	7 Keys To 1000 Times More	8	$10.00 ea	$80.00
38	B-107	The Uncommon Minister Vol. 1	15	$5.00 ea	$75.00
39	B-108	The Uncommon Minister Vol. 2	15	$5.00 ea	$75.00
40	B-114	The Law Of Recognition	5	$10.00 ea	$50.00
41	B-114	The Law Of Recognition	5	$10.00 ea	$50.00
42	B-115	Seeds Of Wisdom On The Secret Place Vol.13	15	$5.00 ea	$75.00
43	B-116	Seeds Of Wisdom On The Holy Spirit Vol.14	15	$5.00 ea	$75.00
44	B-117	Seeds Of Wisdom On The Word Of God Vol.15	15	$5.00 ea	$75.00
45	B-118	Seeds Of Wisdom On Problem Solving Vol.16	15	$5.00 ea	$75.00
46	B-122	Seeds Of Wisdom On Your Assignment Vol.20	15	$5.00 ea	$75.00
47	B-127	Seeds Of Wisdom On Goal-Setting Vol.25	15	$5.00 ea	$75.00
48	B-137	Seeds Of Wisdom On Productivity Vol.27	15	$5.00 ea	$75.00

Total of 445 Books and Display ~~$3,674.00~~
$1,985.00

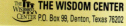 **THE WISDOM CENTER** P.O. Box 99, Denton, Texas 76202

1-888-WISDOM1
(1-888-947-3661)

 Website:
WWW.THEWISDOMCENTER.TV

GIFTS OF WISDOM...
SPECIALTY *Bibles*

*Each Book Sold Separately

- The Businessman's Topical Bible (B-33 / $10)
- The Children's Topical Bible (B-154 / $10)
- The Father's Topical Bible (B-35 / $10)
- The Grandparent's Topical Bible (B-34 / $10)
- The Minister's Topical Bible (B-32 / $10)
- The Mother's Topical Bible (B-36 / $10)
- The New Believer's Topical Bible (B-37 / $10)
- The Seeds of Wisdom Topical Bible (B-31 / $10)
- The ServiceMan's Topical Bible (B-138 / $10)
- The Teen's Topical Bible (B-30 / $10)
- The Traveler's Topical Bible (B-139 / $10)
- The Widow's Topical Bible (B-38 / $10)

The Wisdom Center
Only $10
Wisdom Is The Principal Thing

Add 10% For S/H

J THE WISDOM CENTER 1-888-WISDOM1 Website:
P.O. Box 99, Denton, Texas 76202 (1-888-947-3661) WWW.THEWISDOMCENTER.TV

My Gift Of Appreciation...
The Wisdom Commentary

The Wisdom Commentary includes 52 topics...for mentoring your family every week of the year.

These topics include:

- Abilities
- Achievement
- Anointing
- Assignment
- Bitterness
- Blessing
- Career
- Change
- Children
- Dating
- Depression
- Discipline
- Divorce
- Dreams And Goals
- Enemy
- Enthusiasm
- Favor
- Finances
- Fools
- Giving
- Goal-Setting
- God
- Happiness
- Holy Spirit
- Ideas
- Intercession
- Jobs
- Loneliness
- Love
- Mentorship
- Ministers
- Miracles
- Mistakes
- Money
- Negotiation
- Prayer
- Problem-Solving
- Protégés
- Satan
- Secret Place
- Seed-Faith
- Self-Confidence
- Struggle
- Success
- Time-Management
- Understanding
- Victory
- Weaknesses
- Wisdom
- Word Of God
- Words
- Work

Gift Of Appreciation For Your Sponsorship Seed of $100 or More

y Gift Of Appreciation To My Sponsors! Those Who Sponsor One Square Foot In e Completion Of The Wisdom Center!

nk you so much for becoming a part of this wonderful project...The completion of The Wisdom Center! total purchase and renovation cost of this facility (10,000 square feet) is just over $1,000,000. This is roximately $100 per square foot. **The Wisdom Commentary is my Gift of Appreciation for your nsorship Seed of $100...**that sponsors one square foot of The Wisdom Center. Become a Sponsor! You ove this Volume 1, of The Wisdom Commentary. It is my exclusive Gift of Appreciation for The Wisdom Family who partners with me in the Work of God as a Sponsor.

Add 10% For S/H

THE WISDOM CENTER P.O. Box 99, Denton, Texas 76202

1-888-WISDOM1 (1-888-947-3661)

Website: WWW.THEWISDOMCENTER.TV

UNCOMMON WISDOM FOR UNCOMMON LEADERS

Leadership

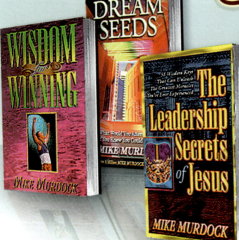

Leadership 4

- **Wisdom For Winning** (B-01 / $10)
- **Dream Seeds** (B-11 / $9)
- **The Leadership Secrets Of Jesus** (B-91 / $10)
- **Wisdom For Crisis Times** (B-40 / $9)

The Wisdom Center
All 4 Books!
Only **$30** $38 Value
WBL-4
Wisdom Is The Principal Thing

Add 10% For S/H

THE WISDOM CENTER
P.O. Box 99, Denton, Texas 76202

1-888-WISDOM1
(1-888-947-3661)

Website:
WWW.THEWISDOMCENTER.TV

L

Master Secrets To Uncommon Increase.

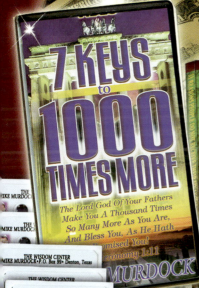

The Wisdom Center
6 Tapes | $30
PAK-008
Wisdom Is The Principal Thing

The Wisdom Center
Free Book
B-82 ($12 Value)
Enclosed!
Wisdom Is The Principal Thing

- The Greatest Success Law I Ever Discovered
- Reasons God Wants To Increase Your Finances
- Important Facts About Obedience

Add 10% For S/H

THE WISDOM CENTER
P.O. Box 99, Denton, Texas 76202

1-888-WISDOM1
(1-888-947-3661)

Website:
WWW.THEWISDOMCENTER.TV

M

The Wisdom Journal

"Write The Things Which Thou Hast Seen, And The Things Which Are, And The Things Which Shall Be Hereafter."
-Revelation 1:19

Stunningly beautiful Black and Gold Leatherette. Contains 160 pages for your personal journaling and diary...a different Wisdom Key for each day...it also includes:

- ▶ 101 Wisdom Keys
- ▶ 31 Facts About Favor
- ▶ 31 Facts About Wisdom
- ▶ 31 Facts About The Holy Spirit
- ▶ 31 Qualities Of An Unforgettable Woman
- ▶ 58 Leadership Secrets Of Jesus
- ▶ Read The Bible Through In A Year Program
- ▶ Sample Page For Effective Note Taking

The Wisdom Center
$20 Each
B-163
Wisdom Is The Principal Thing

Add 10% For S/H

N   THE WISDOM CENTER   P.O. Box 99, Denton, Texas 76202   **1-888-WISDOM1**   **(1-888-947-3661)**   Website: WWW.THEWISDOMCENTER.TV

JOIN THE
Wisdom Key 3000
TODAY!

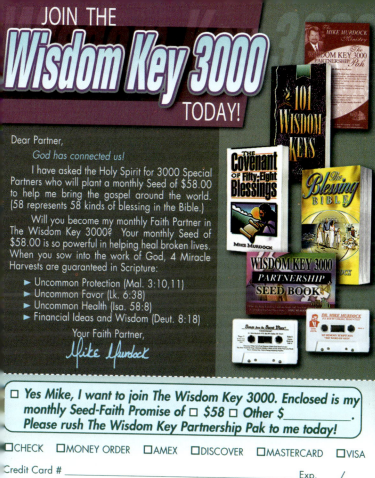

Dear Partner,

God has connected us!

I have asked the Holy Spirit for 3000 Special Partners who will plant a monthly Seed of $58.00 to help me bring the gospel around the world. (58 represents 58 kinds of blessing in the Bible.)

Will you become my monthly Faith Partner in The Wisdom Key 3000? Your monthly Seed of $58.00 is so powerful in helping heal broken lives. When you sow into the work of God, 4 Miracle Harvests are guaranteed in Scripture:

- ▶ Uncommon Protection (Mal. 3:10,11)
- ▶ Uncommon Favor (Lk. 6:38)
- ▶ Uncommon Health (Isa. 58:8)
- ▶ Financial Ideas and Wisdom (Deut. 8:18)

Your Faith Partner,

Mike Murdock

☐ **Yes Mike, I want to join The Wisdom Key 3000. Enclosed is my monthly Seed-Faith Promise of ☐ $58 ☐ Other $_____. Please rush The Wisdom Key Partnership Pak to me today!**

☐ CHECK   ☐ MONEY ORDER   ☐ AMEX   ☐ DISCOVER   ☐ MASTERCARD   ☐ VISA

Credit Card # _____ Exp. ___/___

Signature _____

Name _____ Birth Date ___/___/___

Address _____

City _____ State _____ Zip _____

Phone _____ E-Mail _____

Our Seed-Faith offerings are used to support the Mike Murdock Evangelistic Association, The Wisdom Center and all its programs. The Ministry serves the right to redirect funds as needed in order to carry out our charitable purpose.

Clip and mail completed form to:

THE WISDOM CENTER
P.O. Box 99, Denton, Texas 76202

1-888-WISDOM1
(1-888-947-3661)

Website:
WWW.THEWISDOMCENTER.TV

UNCOMMON WISDOM FOR UNCOMMON ACHIEVERS

Dream 7 PAK

- ► The Leadership Secrets Of Jesus (B-91 / $10)
- ► Dream Seeds (B-11 / $9)
- ► Secrets Of The Richest Man Who Ever Lived (B-99 / $10)
- ► The Assignment; The Dream And The Destiny, Volume 1 (B-74 / $10)
- ► The Holy Spirit Handbook (B-100 / $10)
- ► The Law Of Recognition (B-114 / $10)
- ► 31 Reasons People Do Not Receive Their Financial Harvest (B-82 / $12)

The Wisdom Center
7 Books for only
$50 $71 Value
WBL-23
Wisdom Is The Principal Thing

Add 10% For S/H

P THE WISDOM CENTER
P.O. Box 99, Denton, Texas 76202

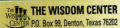
1-888-WISDOM1
(1-888-947-3661)

Website:
WWW.THEWISDOMCENTER.TV